CLASSICS OF PERSONAL DEVELOPMENT

HOW TO MEDITATE

A Guide to Self-Discovery

Lawrence LeShan

Afterword by Edgar N. Jackson

Thorsons
An Imprint of HarperCollins*Publishers*

To Max Grossman,
who taught me that
the opposite of 'injustice' is
not 'justice' but 'love'.

Thorsons
An Imprint of HarperCollins*Publishers*
77–85 Fulham Palace Road,
Hammersmith; London W6 8JB

Originally published in the USA and Canada
Little Brown and Company 1974
First published in the UK by Turnstone Press 1983
Published by Aquarian 1993
This edition 1995

1   3   5   7   9   10   8   6   4   2

© Lawrence LeShan 1974

Lawrence LeShan asserts the moral right to
be identified as the author of this work

A catalogue record for this book
is available from the British Library

ISBN 1 85538 277 6

Printed in Great Britain by
HarperCollinsManufacturing Glasgow

CONTENTS

I would like to express my appreciation to those who have, through their invaluable comments and criticisms, helped me with this book. In particular I thank Joyce Goodrich, Gertrude Schmeidler and Edgar Jackson. The students of my training seminars have, by their honest feedback — both negative and positive — been a very great source of help. Much of the work that made this book possible was done under the auspices of grants from Frederick Ayer II and from the Life Energies Research Foundation. Both of these have my deep gratitude. To Anne Appelbaum, who helped with the search for myself that has made much of this work possible, my gratitude and love. And, profoundly, to Eda LeShan, whose contributions to this work are too many to list, my love.

WHY WE MEDITATE

≈

A few years ago, I was at a small conference of scientists all of whom practised meditation on a daily basis. Toward the end of the four-day meeting, during which each of them had described at some length *how* he meditated, I began to press them on the question of *why* they meditated. Various answers were given by different members of the group and we all knew that they were unsatisfactory, that they did not really answer the questions. Finally one man said, 'It's like coming home.' There was silence after this, and one by one all nodded their heads in agreement. There was clearly no need to prolong the enquiry further.

This answer to the question 'Why meditate?' runs all through the literature written by those who practise this discipline. We meditate to find, to recover, to come back to something of ourselves we once dimly and unknowingly had and have lost without knowing what it was or where or when we lost it. We may call it access to more of our human potential or being closer to ourselves and to reality, or to more of our capacity for love and zest and enthusiasm, or our knowledge that we are a part of the universe and can never be alienated or separated from it, or our ability to see and function in reality more effectively. As we work at meditation, we find that each of these statements of the goal has the same meaning. It is this loss, whose recovery we search for, that led the psychologist Max Wertheimer to define an adult as 'a deteriorated child'.

Eugen Herrigel, who studied the Zen method of meditation for a long time, wrote, 'Working on a KOAN (a meditational technique of that school) leads you to a point where you are behaving like a person trying to remember something you have forgotten.' And Louis Claude de St Martin, summing up *his* reasons for his long years of meditation, succinctly put it, 'We are all in a widowed state and our task is to remarry'.

It is our fullest 'humanhood', the fullest use of what it means to be human, that is the goal of meditation. Meditation is a tough-minded, hard discipline to help us move toward this goal. It is not the invention of any one man or one school. Repeatedly, in many different places and times, serious explorers of the human condition have come to the conclusion that human beings have a greater potential for being, for living, for participation and expression, than they have ability to use. These explorers have developed training methods to help people reach these abilities, and these methods (meditational practices) all have much in common. As I shall show in Chapters 4, 5 and 6, all are based on the same insights and princi-ples, whether they were developed early in India, in the fifth to twelfth century in the Syrian and Jordanian deserts, in tenth-century Japan, in medieval European monasteries, in Poland and Russia in the eighteenth and nineteenth centuries or at other times and places.

All take work. There is no easy or royal road to the goal we seek. Further, there is no end to the search; there is no position from which we can say, 'Now I have arrived, I can stop working.' As we work we find ourselves more at home in the universe, more at ease with ourselves, more able to work effectively at our tasks and toward our goal, closer to our fellow man, less anxious and less hostile. We do not, however, reach an end. As in all serious matters – love, the appreciation of beauty, efficiency – there is no endpoint to the poten-tial of human growth. We work – in meditation – as part of a process; we seek a goal knowing it is forever unattainable.

A good programme of meditation is, in many ways, quite similar to a good programme of physical exercise. Both require repeated hard work. The work is often basically pretty silly in its formal aspect. What could be more foolish than to repeatedly lift twenty pounds up and down unless it is counting your breaths up to four over and over again, a meditational exercise? In both the exercise is for the effect on the person doing it rather than for the goal of lifting lead or counting breaths. Both programmes should be adapted to the particular person using them with the clear understanding that there is no one 'right' programme for everyone. It would be stupid to give the same physical programme to two individuals differing widely in build, general physical condition, and relationship of the development of the breathing and blood circulating apparatus to the development of the muscles. It is equally stupid to give the same meditational programme to two individuals differing widely in the development of the intellectual, emotional and sensory systems and in the relationship of these systems to each other. One of the reasons the formal schools of meditational practice have such a high percentage of failures among their students – those who get little out of the practices and leave meditation completely – is that most schools tend to believe that there is one right way to meditate for everyone and, by a curious coincidence, it happens to be the one they use. Both physical and meditational programmes have, as a primary goal, the tuning and training of the person so that he can effectively move toward his goals.

Does meditation also change these goals? Certainly the increased competence and knowledge of this competence, the increased ability to act whole-heartedly and whole-mindedly, the wider perception of reality and the more coherent personality organization that it brings do change the individual's actions and goals as much as good psychotherapy is likely to change actions and goals for the same reason.

My goals are a function of the way I perceive myself and the world. As these perceptions clarify and broaden, my goals also develop. As I become less anxious and feel less vulnerable, I become less suspicious of and hostile to my fellows, and my goals and actions change. The analogy between physical and meditational programmes cannot be carried too far, but it seems reasonable here to point out that a person who has trained his body and is confident of it feels far less vulnerable than a person with an untrained and unco-ordinated body.

There is no age limit for meditation. This book was originally titled *Meditation for Adults*. One can practise, and benefit from, these disciplines as long as you are adult enough to understand that your own growth and becoming is a serious matter and worth making time for. And so long as you understand that if you wish the best from and for yourself, you will have to work hard, that it does not come without sustained effort.

Meditational techniques have been primarily developed by individuals generally termed 'mystics' and in certain mystical training schools or traditions in which individuals come together to study and practise these techniques. The term 'mystic' has long been widely misunderstood in Western culture as referring to an individual who believes in things no one else can understand, who withdraws from the world and has little to do with its ordinary activities, who talks or writes in terms that communicate nothing and who, if not actually certifiable as insane, has drifted so far from common sense that he certainly could not be considered sane. (There has certainly been a modification of this viewpoint in the past few years in this country, but the position as stated has been the prevailing view for a long time. Recent developments in Western culture are changing this stereotype.)

It is certainly true that there are a good many individuals who identify themselves as mystics who fit these criteria. However, if we look carefully at the larger number of those who are classified or who classify themselves as mystics we find a curiously different picture. We see that the two main characteristics of this group are their high level of efficiency at what they do. (Western mystics are especially noted for their proficiency in business)[1] and the serenity, good human relationships, zest, peace and joy that fill their lives. Further, their agreement on major issues – the nature of man and the universe, the ethical standards of life, and the like – is very strong no matter what time and culture they live in. All mystics, wrote de St Martin, 'come from the same country and speak the same language.' Speaking to this point, C. D. Broad, the British philosopher, has written:

> To me, the occurrence of mystical experience at all times and places, and the similarities between the statements of so many mystics all the world over, seems to be a really significant fact. 'Prima facie' it suggests that there is an aspect of reality with which these persons come in contact and largely fail to describe in the language of daily life. I should say that this 'prima facie' appearance of objectivity ought to be accepted at its face value unless and until some reasonably satisfactory explanation of the agreement can be given.[2]

Evelyn Underhill, herself both a serious mystic and an outstanding student of the literature of mysticism, wrote in this regard:

> The most highly developed branches of the human family have in common one peculiar characteristic. They tend to produce – sporadically it is true, and often in the teeth of adverse external circumstances – a curious and definite type of personality; a type which refuses to be satisfied with that which other men call experience, and is inclined, in the words of its enemies, to 'deny the world in order that it may find reality.' We need these persons in the east and the west; in the ancient, medieval and modern worlds . . . whatever the place or period in which they have arisen, their aims, doctrines and methods have been substantially the same. Their experience, therefore, forms a body of evidence, curiously self-consistent and often mutually explanatory, which must be taken into account before we can add up the sum of the energies and potentialities of the human spirit, or reasonably speculate on its relations to the unknown world which lies outside the boundaries of sense.[3]

Mysticism, from a historical and psychological viewpoint, is the search for and experience of the relationship of the individual himself and the totality that makes up the universe. A mystic is either a person who has this knowledge as background music to his daily experience or else a person who strives and works consistently to attain this knowledge.

The results of this attainment are a capacity to transcend the painful and negative aspects of everyday life and to live with a serenity, an inner peace, a joy and a capacity to love that are so characteristic of the lives of the mystics. The best of mysticism also provides a zest, a fervour and gusto in life plus a much higher ability to function in the affairs of everyday life.

All other definitions of mysticism and mystics are the definitions of one particular school or religious group. They may be adequate definitions for that particular religious group; they are not adequate for the basic meaning of the term.

The mystic regards this search for knowledge of his relationship with the universe (and for a very deep sense of the *union* of himself and the All) as a search for a lost knowledge he once had and for a way of being that is the natural one for man. The root of the word 'mystic' is the same root as the word 'to close'. The mystical search is training in closing off all those artificial factors which ordinarily keep us from this knowledge, this birthright we have lost.

Mystics are individuals who have worked long and hard at meditation and who have had their perception of and their ability to participate in reality changed by the work that they have done. Much of each mystic's *specific* views about reality are coloured by the culture he grew up in, but behind the façade of different terms and specifics, there are deep, vast areas of agreement.

In the classical Western tradition, there are two alternative paths to mystical development in addition to the *via meditativa*, the way of meditation. These are the *via ascetica* and the *via illuminata*.

The *via ascetica*, the way of assault on the body and ego, is of little applicability today. Never very useful in itself, its long years of fasting, self-flagellation, etc., are simply not going to be followed much in Western culture as we know it. The *via illuminata*, the sudden tremendous change in personality integration and understanding, has been the source of some mystic's development. However, it happens so rarely that there is really no point in holding your breath waiting for it. If you are on the right part of the road to Damascus at the right time – congratulations! Otherwise, you had better get to work meditating if you are interested in this sort of growth. In addition, of course, it has been generally reported that followers of both these roads have done a great deal of meditation.

There are two major common results reported by mystics the world over and that all mystical training schools (such as Zen, Hesychasm, Yoga, Sufi, Christian mysticism, Hindu mysticism, Jewish mysticism, and so on) aim toward. These are greater efficiency in everyday life and comprehension of a different view of reality than the one we ordinarily use.

GREATER EFFICIENCY IN EVERYDAY LIFE

Nowhere is the usual stereotype of the mystic as wrong as it is in this area. The mystic is usually seen as unworldly and dreamy. It is a strange concept, almost as if anyone who trained regularly and in a disciplined manner in a gymnasium were to be considered as belonging to a group whose members were regarded as unmuscular and unco-ordinated. Much of the work of any form of meditation is in learning to do one thing at a time: if you are thinking about something to be just thinking of it and nothing else; if you are dancing to be just dancing and not thinking about your dancing. This kind of exercise certainly produces more efficiency at anything we do rather than less.

Tuning and training the mind as an athlete tunes and trains his body is one of the primary aims of all forms of meditation. This is one of the basic reasons that this discipline increases efficiency in everyday life.

There are also other reasons. One of these (I shall discuss others in later chapters) rests on a theory of how to reorganize the personality structure therapeutically. 'If we look deeply into such ways of life as Buddhism or Taoism, Vedanta or Yoga,' wrote Alan Watts, 'we do not find either philosophy or religion as these are understood in the

West. We find something much more nearly resembling psychotherapy.[4] In this area, mysticism and Western psychotherapy follow different paths to the same goal. If I have a severe anxiety attack and go for help to a psychotherapist, he will attempt to aid me primarily by exploring the *content* of the problem: what is it focused on, what is the content of its symbolic meaning on different personality levels? He will work on the theory that as the content is reorganized in a more healthful and positive manner.

If, however, with the same anxiety attack, I go for help to a specialist in meditation, he will attempt to aid me primarily by strengthening and reorganizing the *structure* and ability to function of my personality organization. He will give me various exercises to practise in order to strengthen the overall structure of this organization. He will work on the theory that as the structure is made stronger and more coherent by these exercises, content that is on a nonideal level (e.g., material that is repressed and causing symptoms) will move to preferable levels and will be reorganized properly.

Both theories are valid and both approaches 'work'. Both are also in primitive states of the art and there is a great deal of nonsense at present in both mystical and psychotherapeutic practices. Perhaps ultimately we may hope for a synthesis of the two, combining the best features of each and discarding the concretistic thinking and superstition presently found in both. This would certainly lead to a much more effective method, but unfortunately there is very little research in this direction at present. A few psychologists and psychiatrists – such as Arthur Deikman, M.D. – have been experimenting with this synthesis and doing some excellent work with it. A bare beginning *is* being made.

COMPREHENSION OF ANOTHER VIEW OF REALITY

The second major result reported by mystics of all times and places, and aimed at in their training by all mystical schools, is the comprehension of a different view of reality. I use the term 'comprehension' here to indicate an emotional as well as an intellectual understanding of and participation in this view.

This is a strange and difficult claim. What can the mystic mean when he refers to a different view of reality? Is not reality what is 'out there' and is not our task to understand 'it'? If there are two different views, must not one be 'right' and the other 'wrong'? If the mystic says that there are two equally valid views, is he not speaking in a basic contradiction?

The problem is a real one. On the one hand we *know* our usual view of reality is essentially correct. Not only does it 'feel' right, but we operate in it far too efficiently; the results of our actions are predictable enough so that it is obvious that our assumptions about the nature of reality (on which we base our actions) must be correct.

On the other hand, a large number of serious people – including many of those whom humanity regards very highly – have stated clearly that they were basing their actions on a quite different view of how the world works. They also state that they 'know' this other view to be valid. And, to make it worse, they also appear to achieve their ends, to operate efficiently in the world, often to have a large effect on it. They also claim to have achieved serenity and joy in their lives, and outside observers report that their behaviour appears to bear out this claim.

I shall discuss in some detail this other viewpoint about the nature of reality in Chapter 3. Perhaps it will suffice here to say that if we have learned one thing from modern physics, it is that there may be two viewpoints about something which are mutually contradictory and yet both viewpoints are equally 'correct'. In physics this is called the principle of complimentarity. It states that for the fullest understanding of some phenomena we must approach them from two different viewpoints. Each viewpoint by itself tells only half of the truth.

The mystic does not claim that one way of comprehending reality, of being at home in the universe, is superior to the other. He claims rather that for his fullest humanhood, a person needs both. The Roman mystic Plotinus said man must be seen as an amphibian who needs both life and land and life in the water to achieve his fullest 'amphibianhood'. So, also, man needs to be at home in the world in two different ways – one can call them 'different states of conscious' or 'use of different systems of metaphysics' – for his fullest development. In a curiously similar way, the Indian mystic Ramakrishna likened man to a frog who, in his youth, lives as a tadpole in one medium only. 'Later, however,' wrote Ramakrishna, 'when the tail of ignorance drops off,' he needs in his adulthood *both* land and water for the fullest attainment of his potential.

It is this second way of perceiving reality that is one of the goals of meditation. And, indeed, those who have attained it and gone on to make a working fusion of the two ways, so that one is, at one time, the background music for the other and vice versa, certainly claim and appear to others to be leading much fuller and richer lives than before and than the rest of our race do. Certainly they are also the kind of person it is a pleasure to share our planet with.

These, then, are the goals of meditation. It is indeed a sort of 'coming home'.

In the rest of this book I will discuss the nature of this other view of reality, the basic structure of meditations and the major forms they take, and the psychological and physiological effects of meditation. I will then present detailed instructions for a sample of meditations covering most of the major forms. After that is a section on common errors ('alluring traps') in meditation and mysticism, and a concluding discussion on the value of meditation to the individual and society.

I had originally intended to include a chapter on the major mystical and meditational training schools, such as Yoga, Zen, Sufi and Gurdjieff. However, it soon became plain that it would be foolish to try to abbreviate briefly what has already been done so well and is widely available today. For most of the major schools, the best I could possibly hope for is a very poor man's version of Jacob Needleman's classic, *The New Religions* (New York: Doubleday, 1970). Huston Smith in his *Religions of Man* (New York: Harper & Row, 1958) has covered the major religions far better than I could. For Christian mysticism, Evelyn Underhill's *Mysticism* (New York: E.P. Dutton, 2nd ed., 1930) is still the definitive work. For Hasidic mysticism, Martin Buber's *Tales of the Hasidim* (New York: Schocken, 1967) seems to me to be the best overview. For a first survey of these schools, or if you are considering training in one of them, I would recommend Needleman's *The New Religions*.

Serious meditation is hard work, often frustrating and yet deeply satisfying, and the oldest and newest great adventure for man. I hope it will mean as much to you as it has to me.

HOW A MEDITATION FEELS

Before we discuss why meditation has the effects that it does, the different types of meditation and how to choose the best ones for you (for you as an individual at this specific time in your own development), it is time to try one out in order to get some feel for what we are talking about. We will choose here a basic discipline called Breath Counting.

Counting your breath is a meditation essentially designed to teach and practise the ability to do one thing at a time. It seems simple on the face of it, but do not let its apparent simplicity fool you. It is very hard, requires a great deal of practice, and – if worked at consistently – has definite positive psychological and physiological effects.

Here, however, I suggest that you just try it for fifteen minutes in order to get a sense of what this work feels like. You start by placing yourself in a comfortable position so that you will get as few distracting signals from your body as possible. This may be either sitting, lying on the floor, or standing, depending on your particular wishes. Set an alarm or timer for fifteen minutes or, if this is not available, place a clock-face where you can see it without moving your head. If you use an alarm clock or timer, use one with a gentle sound or muffle it with a pillow.

Now simply count silently each time you breathe out. Count 'one' for the first breath, 'two' for the second, 'three' for the third, 'four' for the fourth, and then start with 'one' again. Keep repeating this procedure until the fifteen minutes are up.

The goal is to be doing simply that and nothing more. If other thoughts come in (and they will), simply accept the fact that you are straying from the instructions and bring yourself gently and firmly back to the counting. No matter what other thoughts, feelings or perceptions come during the fifteen minutes, your task is simply to keep counting your breaths, to keep trying to be doing *only* that. Doing or being conscious of anything else during this period is wandering away from the task. (These instructions are repeated in more detail in Chapter 8, but these directions are sufficient for our task at the moment.)

Do not expect to do well at it, to be able to succeed for more than a couple of seconds at a time in being aware only of your counting. That takes long practice. Simply do your best.

Now begin!

The road of meditation is not an easy one. The first shock of surprise comes when you realize how undisciplined our mind really is; how it refuses to do the bidding of our will. After fifteen minutes of attempting only to count our breaths and not to be thinking of anything else, we realize that if our bodies were half as unresponsive to our will as our minds are, we would never get across a street alive. We find ourselves thinking of all sorts of other things rather than the simple thing we have just decided to think about. Saint Teresa of Avila once described the mind of man as an 'unbroken horse that would go anywhere except where you wanted it to.'

Plato also wrote of this problem. He likened the mind of man to a ship on which the sailors had mutinied and locked the Captain and the Navigator below in the cabin. The sailors believe themselves to be perfectly free and steer the ship as they feel like at each moment. First one sailor steers for a while, then another, and the ship travels in erratic and random directions since the sailors can neither agree on a goal nor navigate the ship toward it if they could agree. The task of a human being, wrote Plato, is to quell the mutiny, to release the Captain and the Navigator so that there can be the freedom to choose a goal and to steer (work) consistently and coherently toward its attainment. Only in this situation when one is free of the tyranny of the whim of the moment can there be real freedom.

A curiously similar analogy is found in the Bhagavad-Gita, a long poem with much attention to meditation and mysticism written in India between the second and fifth centuries B.C.:

> *The wind turns a ship*
> *From its course upon the waters:*
> *The wandering winds of the senses*
> *Cast man's mind adrift*
> *And turn his better judgement from its courses.*
> *When a man can still his senses*
> *I call him illumined.*

But quelling the mutiny Plato wrote of takes long, hard, consistent work. The sailors reject and evade the discipline with a variety of devices. As we seriously work at a meditation, perhaps we find ourselves becoming sleepy, bored, thinking of all sorts of other things, creative, at work on another problem, hallucinating all sorts of interesting perceptions and sensations, solving old problems, and God knows what else, as the 'unbroken horse' of Saint Teresa does everything possible to refuse to be disciplined to our will. This may even include sensations of being flooded with intense white light and the curious belief that you have attained 'enlightenment' and know the truth about everything. Thomas Merton, who knew a very great deal about meditation, wrote of this last type of experience and the attitude that follows it:

> *. . . some people become convinced that the mystical life must be something like Wagnerian opera. Tremendous things keep happening all the time. Every new motion of the spirit is heralded by thunder and lightning. The heavens crack open and the soul sails upward out of the body into a burst of unearthly and splendid light. There it comes face to face with God, in the midst of a huge 'Turnverein' of flying, singing, trumpet-playing saints and angels. There is an eloquent exchange of views between the soul and God in*

an operatic duet that lasts at least seven hours, for seven is a mystical number. All this is punctuated by earthquakes, solar and lunar eclipses and the explosion of super-substantial bombs. Eventually, after a brief musical preview of the end of the world and the Last Judgement, the soul pirouettes gracefully back into the body and the mystic comes to himself to discover that he is surrounded by a hushed, admiring circle of fellow religious, including one or two who are surreptitiously taking down notes of the event in view of some future process of canonization. [1]

Merton here is writing of one of the major blocks in our culture to meditational practices and inner development. This is the belief that whatever happens, happens suddenly and startlingly, and that if a meditation or a particular meditational discipline does not produce these results, it should be discontinued and another one started. It is out of this type of belief that we get the 'spiritual athletes' so prevalent among those interested in this kind of work today. They express their lack of discipline by repeatedly shifting from one type of meditational work to another, according to the fad of the moment, and believe that they are quelling the mutiny in their interior ships at the very moment that they are encouraging its victory. To return to our analogy of the gymnasium, we do not expect to work and work at the weights with no changes in our body until all at once our muscles pop up, our stomach flattens, and we look like Tarzan or Raquel Welch. We expect a rather long, slow, generally imperceptible process of change in the direction we wish. The same is true of meditation.

One of the reasons given for this lack of discipline and the shifting from one fad to another – as Paris dictates the fad of the moment in women's clothing, Esalen Institute in California dictates the fad of the moment in meditation – is the accounts given in books on Zen of what happens to Zen students when they have worked enough with the Koan technique. Suddenly, the reports go, they comprehend the answer, start to tremble, and sweat profusely. The master then agrees they have found the answer to this problem, solved (worked enough with) this particular meditation. This is frequently interpreted by the reader (and sometimes by the Zen students) as meaning that they have 'achieved enlightenment' and the reader closes the book with a deep sigh of envy and hope. However, if, instead of closing the book, he turned to the next page, he would notice that the student then received the next Koan to work with and his meditations continued. There is no more talk of 'enlightenment', his work continues.

Cardinal Newman wrote that there are no real sudden conversions, but that sometimes there is a sudden realization that you are what you have already become through hard work.

The belief that 'enlightenment' occurs suddenly and completes the whole task when it happens is curiously similar to the belief in 'insight' in the early days of psychotherapy. At that time it was felt that a patient worked with a problem until he suddenly achieved insight into its structure and meaning. He then had a profound emotional experience (no 'great white lights', but just about everything else that is told of in mystical literature about enlightenment experiences) and the problem was solved.

Alas. Long hard experience in psychotherapy has taught us that this is not so. True, insight experiences fitting the description occur (as do enlightenment experiences), but they are only the beginning. They, by themselves, rarely change much. After the insight comes the long hard work of following it up: of changing our perceptions, feelings and behaviour to gradually, painfully, bring them into accord with our understanding. As we have had to give up our hope for sudden major personality changes during psychotherapy, we have also had to give them up in meditational practices.

3

THE PSYCHOLOGICAL EFFECTS OF MEDITATION

In Chapter 1, I described the two major psychological effects of consistent meditation: the attainment of another way of perceiving and relating to reality and a greater efficiency and enthusiasm in everyday life. This chapter is an attempt to explain why meditation has these effects and to say something more about them. In order to explain the why it is necessary to make a diversion into the history of physics and into philosophy and to cover some fairly complex material. This chapter, therefore, is the most difficult one in the entire book and if you are not particularly interested in this specific subject you can skip to page 25 without any especially serious loss.

The reason for the excursion into the history of physics is that one segment of this history displays a clear parallel to what happens to the individual in serious meditation. There arose a problem that had to be solved, but it could not be solved by thinking about it in the usual way. It became necessary, therefore, to develop a new way of thinking about reality in order to solve it. In meditation, also, a problem arises that cannot be solved in our usual ways of thinking about and relating to the world and it becomes necessary to develop a new way of doing these things in order to solve it. Let us look first at the history of physics.

At the turn of the twentieth century, the field of theoretical physics was in a shambles. The Michaelson-Morley experiment had presented data which simply could not be interpreted in any way that made sense. The 'addition of velocities' problem this experiment posed could not be solved by the usual ways of thinking about and solving problems in science.

The essence of the Michaelson-Morley experiment – and it was repeated many times – demonstrated absolutely that there were situations in which 2 plus 2 did not make 4! It concerned the speed of light and presented clear evidence that the speed of light approaching its target remained the same no matter how rapidly you moved its source toward or away from the target. To say the least, these were startling results that simply could not fit with the scientific understanding of the time. They were, however, too clear to be ignored.

Out of the pressure created by this paradox, physics developed a new way of perceiving reality. The concept of perceiving the world as working on a different metaphysical system than the usual mechanical view had been stated in physics for a long time. We might call this other picture of how the world works the 'field theory' view of reality. It was first clarified and demonstrated by that great genius of physics Clerk Maxwell. However, except in specialized fields (such as hydrodynamics), little had been done with it. It remained for Einstein to generalize it to *all* of reality and to demonstrate that it was a valid way of conceptualizing what is.

For our purposes, the crucial aspect of this history is the fact that a paradox that could not be solved and yet had to be solved forced a new way of understanding reality into being.[1]

Most meditations pose an impossible paradox. They force the individual to transcend his usual everyday way of perceiving, thinking about and relating to the world and himself in order to 'solve' the paradox. Thus, as in the history of physics, a new way of being in, conceptualizing and relating to reality and himself is forced to emerge.

As I have described elsewhere,[2] the view of reality we are forced to by serious meditation is the same view that physics was forced to by the impossible situation developed as a result of the Michaelson-Morley experiment. The difference between the two is that physicists were only forced to accept the new view intellectually and could do this with relative comfort from behind a screen of mathematics. The meditator is forced to the full emotional acceptance as well as the intellectual acceptance of the validity of this viewpoint and the process may be, and often is, decidedly less comfortable.

In what way does serious meditation force us to grow beyond our usual view of how the world works and to accept that there is another equally valid and important view? In 1900, the academic philosopher Josiah Royce, writing with the beautiful limpidity we associate with Plato, published a little book entitled *The Conception of Immortality*.[3] In it he demonstrates that our usual ways of reacting, perceiving, thinking, analyzing cannot really deal with the idea of individuality. All things, qualities, traits, etc., are seen as part of a class in comparison to or in relation to other things, qualities, etc.; strive as we will we cannot find a quality in ourselves or others that we consider by itself, not in relation to the absence, presence or amount of it in others. And yet, points out Royce, we *know* that there is something individual about each person. In a stunning demonstration, he points out that if we are in love with someone we know deeply that they are completely individual and irreplaceable by anyone else in the universe. Yet, try as we will, we cannot describe in what this individuality lies because all our effort and ability succeed only in describing amounts of traits or aspects that other individuals also have, and so there could well be – in spite of our knowledge that this is not so – another person somewhere with exactly the same percentages of each trait who could replace our loved one with no loss to us.

Just as physics could not, with its usual commonsense picture of the world, solve a problem and had to grow to include a new picture, so our usual, commonsense minds and ways of picturing the world cannot solve the problem of individuality, and, if forced hard enough to concentrate on this problem, they will grow to the comprehension of a new world picture, a new metaphysical system.

Now we begin to see how meditation works toward this end. A formal, or 'structured', meditation is both a *way* of thinking about or perceiving one thing at a time and a *training device* to help us to be able to do this in other contexts. (An informal or 'unstructured' meditation consists in thinking in much more our usual ways about a particular subject until we understand it more deeply.) As we continue to work with a meditation of this sort over a long period of time, two things happen. First, the work itself strengthens the personality organization until we are structurally strong enough to bear the shock of the new viewpoint of how reality is put together. Second, we will find ourselves working past the tremendous number of self-created distractions – including long dry periods when our inner life, in Thomas Merton's phrase, 'seems like a desert' – and beginning to perceive just one thing at a time, considered in itself in our consciousness without comparisons or relationships. At that time we will also begin to grow toward the new comprehension of a way of being in the world, of a new way of perceiving and relating to reality. As we comprehend more and more of this, we find that we are coming home to long-lost parts of ourselves, that our zest, vitality, efficiency, capacity to love and relate increase and deepen. We also begin to *know* that each part of us is a part of all others, that no one walks alone, and that we are indeed at home in, and a part of, the universe; to know that, in Giordano Bruno's phrase, 'out of the world we cannot fall'; to know that this world, this universe, is a good home for man.

Is this new way of perceiving and relating to reality an illusion? Is not the usual, 'practical', everyday way the only *real* way? This question inevitably arises as one is introduced to this concept.

Part of the answer comes from the kind of people who have attained this view. By and large they hardly seem to be the kind of people who would be deluding themselves. They represent some of the most important figures in human history, people who have had a marked effect on the rest of us. Here are Socrates and Buddha, and Jesus of Nazareth, Meister Eckhart and George Fox, Lao-tzu and Confucius, Bernard of Clairvaux and the Baal Shem Tov, Rumi, Saint Teresa of Avila and Saint John of the Cross. They tended to be highly efficient administrators, outstanding in business, the arts and professions. Whatever else they were, they were tough-minded and hard-headed.

A second answer comes from what modern physics has been able to do with this metaphysical system. The ideas of Einstein, Planck, Bohr, Heisenberg, Margenau and the other leading physicists of our time on the validity of this view have led us to the ability to accomplish hitherto undreamed of feats. Although these feats have so far chiefly been used in horror and terror, their promise for the future also holds much that is positive. At any rate, atomic energy rests on the fact that a 'field-theory' view of the universe is considered valid by physicists. And this view of how the world works as held by physicists cannot be differentiated from the similar view held by mystics who have arrived at it through meditational discipline.[4] The meditational route to this view has led to increased efficiency, zest, serenity and capacity to love on the part of its practitioners. The theoretical route has led to much greater ability to affect physical reality. On the basis of these successes, it certainly does not look as if the new view of reality is illusory.

One psychological effect of serious meditation, then, is to comprehend a new way of perceiving and relating to the world. On the basis of the experience of those who have achieved it, this attainment, and the path to it, bring a strong serenity and inner peace that remain stable even in the face of much adversity.

The second psychological effect grows out of the work itself. For this effect it is not so important how well you do at a meditation (how effectively you are doing that particular meditation and not thinking of anything else), but rather how hard you work at the job. It is the steady work in which one gently, firmly and consistently beings oneself back to the task at hand that strengthens the will, purpose, goal-oriented behaviour, ability to bar distractions, etc., and facilitates the personality reorganization that is part of our slow, endless growth to real maturity. It is also this consistent work that increases our ability to give ourselves whole-heartedly and completely to whatever we are doing at the moment and increases our ability to cope with a variety of situations and our increased feelings of competence. Experience has shown that those who stay with this kind of work have increased competence and confidence.

One of the differences between meditation and such drugs as LSD, psilocybin, mescaline and other hallucinogens is this: Both drugs and meditation may bring you to this new, 'field-theory' view of reality. However, meditation (if done with reasonable intelligence) does not get you there until you are strong enough to handle it and able to integrate this new way and grow from the integration. The chemical routes bring you there, ready or not, and it is much more unlikely that you will grow through the experience. In addition, the drugs often bring 'bad trips' as they force you to a place you are not ready for or trained to be in. The long-term personality evolution produced by meditation (as opposed to the short-term personality revolution produced by drugs) does not produce bad trips.

Arthur Deikman (a psychiatrist who knows a great deal about meditation) sees meditation as leading to 'deutomatization of perception and behaviour.'

> *Briefly, automatization is assumed to be a basic process in which the repeated exercise of an action or of a perception results in the disappearance from consciousness of its intermediate steps. Deutomatization is the undoing of automatization presumably by reinvestment of action and percepts with attention.*

> *. . . deutomization is not a regression, but rather an undoing of a pattern in order to permit a new and perhaps more advanced experience. The crayfish sloughs its rigid shell when more space is needed for growth. The mystic, through meditation, may also cast off, temporarily, the shell of automatic perception, of automatic affective and cognitive controls in order to perceive more deeply into reality.[5]*

One can see from this definition the reason for the remarkable freshness and clarity of perception that often arises after serious meditational work. Things seem to have more 'suchness'. Red is redder, water is wetter, and mud is muddier. We see again the fresh eyes from which the scales of inattention have dropped. Again and again my students have described seeing the commonplace in a new and alive manner in which everything has a vital and brilliant identity, a luminous quality. The same type of perception has been described so often in mystical literature that it must be accepted that this is a frequent result of the 'cleansing of the gates of perception', through meditation.

These, then, are the twin goals of meditation and of the mystical path: the attainment of a second way of comprehending reality and the increased serenity and competence in being. The fact of attaining a second view of reality, however, does not mean that the two views are then kept separate. This would lead to a greater fragmentation of personality rather than a greater coherence and organization of it. The two views are, in continued work, integrated so that each serves as background to the other. The knowledge of our differences and separateness is clarified and strengthened by the knowledge, held at the same time, of our oneness, that we are each a part of each other. This is one of the lessons of the magnificent Rodin statues that shade from the acutely perceptive analysis of the specialness of the subject into more and more unfinished stone until we seem to be dealing with the raw material of the planet. The thrust, individuality and vibrancy of our perception of the individual person are heightened by our perception of the oneness we share with him as we both shade into the whole planet, all others and the total universe.

In the previous chapter I raised the question of whether meditation changes our goals in life. To the answer to this question given there I must now add another that arises when we are working at this fusion of the two ways of perceiving. If I *know* that you and I are both one, that we are not separated, and that I am not only my brother's keeper, but also my brother, I will treat you as I treat myself. Further, since I know that I am a part of the total cosmos, of all Being, I will treat myself and, therefore, you as something precious. The ethical and behavioural orientations that emerge naturally and originally during the practice of meditation are agreed upon by all serious students of the discipline.

In all good psychotherapy and in all good meditation, there is a therapeutic factor which is rarely mentioned. It is the careful paying attention to ourselves, to *all* of ourselves including those parts we have characterized as 'best' and 'worst'. In this orientation we train ourselves to regard ourselves seriously and to be concerned with our total being, involving not only our best possible relationships with ourselves, but also our best possible relationships with others, which we begin to realize is a deep need of ours and a need that is a part of our total being. In learning to take ourselves seriously we begin to learn how important it is that we garden and cultivate that being and, therefore, by necessity, the being of others.

There is no endpoint to the possibilities of growth and development offered by serious disciplined work with oneself, whether it be by meditation, psychotherapy or by other routes. As in all serious things – in the ability to love, in knowledge and understanding, in the ability to express ourselves, in the appreciation of beauty, or in religious awe – there is always room for more. One of the great medieval mystics, Meister Eckhart, wrote, 'There is no stopping place in this life, – no, nor was there ever for any man no matter how far along his way he'd gone. This above all, then, be ready at all times for the gifts of God, and always for new ones.'

THE PHYSIOLOGICAL EFFECTS
OF MEDITATION

At the present time we are just learning about the effects of meditation on the workings of the body. The new tools of science are now being applied to this area and a good deal of new research is now underway. There are, however, real problems in this sort of research. For example, how do you decide who is an expert meditator and which schools of meditation do you investigate? It is partly for these reasons – as well as a general lack of interest on the part of the scientific community in the past – that so little research has been done. With the increased interest in this field now arising in the West, however, a rather large number of studies have got underway. So far, the majority of them are either on Zen monks (all of whom have serious training in the same type of meditation) or on students of Transcendental Meditation. This last is the work of the Mantra type (see page 58), taught in a standardized, easily learned manner. Due to the rapid growth of this serious school of meditation, there are a good many students available for study. Since these include many professional scientists, the amount of research being done is even larger. Since so much is being done now and because this is a new field, any report of physiological changes due to meditation soon becomes outdated. However, the evidence is clear on certain general relationships between serious meditation and physiological response.

Essentially, meditation seems to produce a physiological state of deep relaxation coupled with a wakeful and highly alert mental state. There tends to be a lower metabolic rate and decreases in heart and respiration rates. The pattern of physiological response to meditation is different from the pattern of response to sleep or hypnosis. The physiological state brought about by meditation appears to be the opposite one from the state brought about by anxiety or anger. Technically, meditation seems to bring about a hypometabolic state that is quite the opposite to the 'defence-alarm' state described by W. B. Cannon when he analysed the physiologic state of the 'flight or fight' reaction.

Central to the response to meditation is the lowered rate of metabolism, the lowered rate of using oxygen and producing carbon dioxide. That these decreases are due to a lowered metabolic rate rather than to a slower or shallower breathing is shown by the fact that both decrease equally and the ratio between them remains the same. This would not be true if it were due to alterations in respiration. There is also typically, in meditation, a slowing of the heartbeat (in one study averaging about three beats per minute) and a decrease in the rate and volume of respiration.

The lactate concentration of the blood decreases sharply during meditation, nearly four times as fast as it does in people resting quietly stretched out in a safe, quiet situation. Blood-lactate level is related to anxiety and tension, and the low level found in subjects during meditation is very likely related to the relaxed state of the meditators.[1]

The resistance of the skin to mild electric current in any individual has long been known to be closely related to the amount of tension and anxiety present. The more tension and anxiety, the lower the skin resistance. In meditation the skin resistance increases, sometimes as much as four hundred per cent. The heartbeat tends to slow down. There also tend to be changes in the pattern of brainwaves. The most usual report of these changes is an increase of slow alpha waves (eight to nine per second).

In hypnosis there is no change in the metabolic rate. During sleep the consumption of oxygen decreases appreciably only after several hours, and then this is due to a decrease in breathing rather than a change in the general rate of metabolism.

Brainwave patterns during sleep are entirely different from those of meditation. In hypnosis the brainwave pattern tends to resemble the pattern typical of whatever state of mind has been suggested to the subject. This is also true of respiration rate, blood pressure, heart rate and skin resistance; in hypnosis these resemble those typically found in the suggested state: there is no pattern typical of hypnosis itself.

Why does your body respond in this way during meditation? There is still a great deal we do not know, though research now underway will very likely fill in some of the gaps. One factor, however, seems to be related to the basic aspect of meditation: that is a focusing on, a doing of one thing at a time. The signals our body gets as to how it should be responding are simpler and more coherent during meditation than at almost any other time.

If we think about the signals we are sending to ourselves at most times of our daily life, we see that they are varied indeed. If I am talking to someone, I am usually not only talking, I am also thinking about where the conversation is going, what has already been said, how I feel about the person I am communicating with, and what the time is. In the background of my thoughts are memories of the earlier parts of the day and plans or concerns for the later parts. In addition, I am conscious of my posture, the feelings of my body, my fatigue level, and whether or not I have a drink or cigarette in my hand or want one. Each of these aspects of my mental activity is sending signals to my physiological apparatus as to the general state of things and how to respond. Each of these signals is different. In meditation we are in the state – or moving toward it – of sending only one set of signals at a time. The effect of this on our physiology is positive and there is a strong tendency to normalize reactions, to behave physiologically in a more relaxed and healthy manner. Tension and anxiety indicators are reduced and our metabolic rate and heartbeat slow. There is an increase in mental awareness and alertness and a decrease in physiological tension.

THE BASIC TYPES OF MEDITATION

There are a great many types of meditation. I shall in this chapter, very briefly, describe the four major classes that most of them fit into. A good number of meditations are combination meditations, falling into more than one of these classes, but before these can be intelligently discussed it is necessary to understand the general classes themselves.

Instead of calling these 'classes of meditation', we might with good reason call them 'paths of meditation'. They answer the question 'What route is followed by this particular practice to attain the goals described in the previous three chapters?' I shall describe the four major routes as: the path through the intellect; the path through the emotions; the path through the body; the path through action.

How does the individual choose which path to follow? There are no absolute rules. Starting with the area you personally feel strongest and most secure in is often the best way. Later, after having worked seriously on this route, you may wish to change to or combine it with another. All lead to the same place eventually. All are hard. Where you are *now*, before you start, is important. The task is difficult enough without making it harder by beginning with your weakest area. Which path *feels* most natural for you as an individual? Start with this one and stay with it for the months necessary to determine if you have made a mistake or if you have chosen correctly.

One teacher of the mystic way, Rabbi Nahman of Bratislava,

wrote, 'God chooses one man with a shout, another with a song, another with a whisper.'

There is one additional test of a meditation or a meditation programme that should always be kept in mind. It generally should make you feel better when you do it than when you do not do it. After each meditation, sit for a few minutes with no particular programme. Just let yourself 'be' for this time (about ten to twenty per cent of the time you actually spend on the meditation). Then ask yourself how you feel compared to how you felt before you started the meditation. If the work you are doing is the right kind of work for you, then most of the time the answer will be that you feel better, more 'put together', more of one piece and less fragmented. If this response does not usually occur, then do not continue with this meditation. If you persevere with the meditation programme which is 'right' for you, then after a month or so you will find yourself becoming 'addicted to feeling good' and will find your motivation increasing to continue this work regularly.

THE PATH THROUGH THE INTELLECT

The path of the intellect appears to many people, and to many mystics, to be a contradiction in terms. It uses the intellect to go beyond the intellect, the will, and directed thought processes to transcend themselves. We consistently pursue thought to provide a revolution in the very heart of thought. This is again similar to the paradoxical situation confronting physics earlier in this century when, in Werner Heisenberg's words, it came to 'the completely unexpected realization that a consistent pursuit of classical physics forces a transformation in the very basis of this physics.'[1]

This path has been followed by a wide variety of mystics. As examples we might mention Jnana Yoga in the East and Habad Hasidism in the Hebrew tradition.

The basic structure of the path of the intellect is that the student first reaches an intellectual understanding of the two realities, the two ways of perceiving and relating to the world, and then, by a series of training exercises – meditations – deepens this understanding. At the same time he is strengthening his personality structure by the discipline. By the use of structured meditations forcing his mind to do what is impossible in our usual ways of perceiving and thinking (see Chapter 3), he completes the process. These three parts of the intellectual path combine to force his understanding of the two ways of relating to reality to become a total organismic comprehension. In the Bhagavad-Gita, this is the first of the paths taught by Krishna to Arjuna. In the modern Eastern tradition we see it most clearly in the approach of Krishnamurti.

The path of the intellect was brought into Christian mysticism largely by Richard of St Victor (died ca. 1173). In the Hebrew tradition, we have this approach in Habad Hadism. Habad is an acronym of three words: Hokmah (wisdom), Binah (intelligence), and Daat (knowledge). The orientation of this training school is clear from this.

For many Westerners, particularly perhaps for intellectuals, this may be the path of choice. It can provide an accustomed method of working at the beginning of the path so that a sense of rightness and security is built up by the time the harder and more upsetting parts of the work are reached.

THE PATH THROUGH THE EMOTIONS

The path through the emotions has probably been the most widely followed of all the mystical paths. The Christian monastic who spends years practising his devotions, ceaselessly working at his ability to love, to feel, to accept, expand and express his *Caritas*, his caring, is on this route. So is the student of Bhakti-Yoga in the East. The Sufi poet Rumi wrote, 'The astrolabe of the mysteries of God is love.' There was an insistence on the part of Baal Shem Tov (the founder of Hasidic mysticism) on the importance of love and feeling in approaching the One. The Eastern follower of this route with the most influence on the West today is probably Meher Baba. Some mystics have felt that this was the *only* valid path. Such was the anonymous author of *The Cloud of Unknowing*. A medieval mystical document, who wrote of God, 'By love He may be gotten and holden, but by thought or understanding, never.'

The path through the emotions concentrates on meditations that loosen the feelings and expand the ability to relate to others, to care and to love. Unstructured meditations (see page 68) are used more by the follower of this path than by those who follow other routes. The basic theory held by meditational schools of this kind (and by nearly all others) is that the more free, untroubled and complete a human being is, the more he has overcome the stunting of his growth due to his cultural training and early experiences, the more he will naturally love and the better he will relate to others. Some meditational schools concentrate on learning to love the self, some on learning to love others, some on learning to love God. Ultimately all arrive at the same place, loving all three. From the mystic's viewpoint there is no separation between self, others and God, and learning to fully care for one leads to full caring for all.

THE ROUTE OF THE BODY

Until quite recently this route has been very little used in the West. Following it, one learns to be aware of one's body and bodily movements and to heighten this awareness through practice until, during the period of meditation, this awareness completely fills the field of consciousness to the exclusion of anything else. Practised consistently it leads to the same results as do the other routes. The best known Eastern forms are Hatha Yoga, T'ai Chi and the Dervish dances of the Sufi mystical tradition. In recent years two Western forms, the Gindler and Alexander methods of sensory awareness have been developed.

A dervish told Nikos Kazantzakis, 'We bless the Lord by dancing . . . Because dancing kills the ego, and once the ego has been killed, there is no further obstacle to prevent you from joining with God.'

There is the Hasidic tale of the great Rabbi who was coming to visit a small town in Russia. It was a very great event for the Jews in the town and each thought long and hard about what questions they would ask the wise man. When he finally arrived, all were gathered in the largest available room and each was deeply concerned with the questions they had for him. The Rabbi came into the room and felt the great tension in it. For a time he said nothing and then began to hum softly a Hasidic tune. Presently all there were humming with him. He then began to sing the song and all were singing with him. Then he began to dance and soon all present were caught up in the dance with him. After a time all were deeply involved in the dance, all fully committed to it, all just dancing and nothing else. In this way, each one became whole with himself, each healed the splits within himself which kept him from understanding. After the dance went on for a time, the Rabbi gradually slowed it to a stop, looked at the group, and said, 'I trust that I have answered all your questions.'

In the complete absorption in one's bodily integration and bodily movement, the meditator is brought slowly and gradually to doing just one thing at a time. This, as in the other routes, integrates and strengthens the personality organization and brings one both the readiness and the need for developing a new way of perceiving and responding to reality. Further, this particular path integrates the different bodily aspects with each other and with the personality in particular.

THE PATH OF ACTION

The path of action consists of learning how to 'be' and to perceive and relate to the world during the performance of a particular type of skill. This approach has been most widely used in the East. Various skills have been used: archery, flower arrangement, aikido and karate (two methods of unarmed combat) in the Zen tradition, and rug weaving in the Sufi tradition. Singing and prayer have been used in the Christian tradition.[2]

Perhaps one of the clearest statements of this path in Christianity is in *The Little Way* of Saint Thérèse of Lisieux. Her way consisted of doing all the small tasks of everyday life with the knowledge that each one is a part of the total harmony of the universe. They were done with love and *with total concentration* and the attitude that this task was the most important thing to be doing at that moment.

As one learns the mystic's way of being in the world during the performance of a specific skill, the long, hard practise disciplines and strengthens the personality. The pure concentration on doing what you are doing and being aware of nothing else is again the impossible task for our everyday way of being, and so the new way is gradually forced into conscious existence. Just as the effect of doing an intellectually-oriented or a bodily-oriented meditation has, over a period of time, an impact on the rest of your daily perceptions and actions, so also does the effect of action-oriented meditations tend to spread out to the rest of your life. It goes without saying that you become quite expert at the particular skills you work with, but this is not the real goal of the work. The real goal is to help you grow and develop as a total human being, not to become a better archer or karate expert. There is no particular reason to suppose that Zen-trained archers are better or worse archers than those who have not used the Zen way-of-action discipline, but have spent an equivalent amount of time practising with bow and arrow. (There is no particular evidence either to show that the Zen-trained archers are *worse* than their otherwise equally trained colleagues.) However, the Zen-trained archers have developed their personality organizations in a way the other archers have not.

This has been a very brief discussion of the major 'route' of mystical training. As I shall describe in Chapters 7 and 10, many meditations are combinations of different routes and most schools of meditation include more than one of these paths. Each person should find the combination of routes best suited to him as an individual. There is no one 'best' way for all; there is a best way for each individual. Sex or age is not a factor. For example, the way of the body can be followed by individuals of any age through sensory awareness or the Alexander method. Each person must find his own best programme depending on his own personality structure. You try to get a sense of how you would feel best working as you are now, not as you would like to be. A programme is built with your present reality as its base. Then stay with each meditation you try for the several weeks necessary to really learn how to use it. At the end of that time, if you feel better *after* you do it than you did before, continue. Otherwise, experiment further.

There is one warning sign in meditation that should always be obeyed. This is a sense that you should not be doing this particular meditation, that it is 'wrong' for you. It is a clear feeling that what you are doing does not fit well with the structure of your being and is damaging or deforming it in some way. When and if (it is quite rare) you have this sense about what you are doing, stop doing it.

I am not speaking about anxiety. If you feel anxious during a meditation, you will probably act as you usually do in other situations when you are anxious: some people stop doing whatever they are doing at the moment and re-evaluate the situation; some people plunge ahead. Personally, since I do not believe in heroics in personal growth, I recommend the first course, but each person will make his own choice.

I am speaking of a definite and clear feeling that you are doing something to yourself that you should not be doing. Always obey this warning. Stop the meditation you are doing and do not resume it until at least several months have passed and you understand fully the reasons you felt that way and that these reasons no longer exist. By and large, if a meditation makes you feel that it is doing you harm, you are never going to get much out of working with it. You might just as well let it go completely and use other forms of meditation. I have never heard of anyone having this feeling when doing Breath Counting or Contemplation. However, it does happen, rarely, with other forms of this work.

In any serious meditation programme there will be dry, dull periods when you just feel bored with the work. These feelings are part of your resistance. Stay with it, if you can, during these periods. Work *harder* at it. Presently it will pass (as it becomes apparent to you that this method of resisting discipline does not work) and you will find the meditation a deeper, richer experience at the end of the dry period than it was before.

Although 'discipline' and 'will' have become, for many people today, trigger words that they immediately respond to negatively, they are necessary in understanding meditation. One student of meditation asked me, 'How do I keep bringing my mind back to the breath counting?' He looked quite surprised, for a moment, when I said, 'By means of your active will.' After thinking about my answer for a moment, he was quite satisfied with it.

The Bhagavad-Gita puts it plainly: 'Patiently, little by little, a man must free himself from all mental distractions, with the aid of the intelligent will.'

If you are one of the people who immediately respond negatively to terms like 'discipline' and 'will', it might be interesting for you to ask yourself 'why?'

STRUCTURED AND UNSTRUCTURED MEDITATIONS

In this chapter I will describe some ways of looking at mental meditations, meditations you do essentially 'in your head', that is, without bodily movement. The fact that we term these 'mental' does not mean that they do not also effect the emotional life and the physiology of the body. It simply means that they do not involve the use of the muscular apparatus. You do them while remaining in one position.

First let us discuss the difference between 'structured' and 'unstructured' meditations. A structured meditation is one that carefully and precisely defines what the inner activity is that you are working toward. Breath Counting, as described in Chapter 2, is a structured meditation. The instructions are to count your breaths up to four and then to start again. You are to keep trying to be aware only of this counting and every time you begin to think of, or be aware of, anything else, to bring yourself back gently and firmly to the counting. The instructions are very precise as to *what* you are to do. Similarly, the Lotus meditation (described in Chapter 8) is a structured meditation. After choosing a subject one thinks about it in an exactly defined manner. Any straying from this precise manner is not following the meditation and is corrected as soon as you become aware of your wandering.

As you have seen from the experience with Breath Counting, this is extremely hard and rigorous work. It takes constant attention and vigilance. Its goal is an all-out effort to follow the directions completely and coherently from your toes to your hair. Further, the deeper we get into it, the more we practise it and the more expert at it we become, the more we see that it is impossible to do completely without some real expansion of the ways we can perceive and relate to reality. It is just not possible, in our usual, everyday way of being, to think actively and dynamically of just one thing at a time without comparisons or classes of things, and yet it is exactly this task which the directions of the meditation tell us must be done. Faced with an impossible task, and working in a hard, disciplined manner toward its accomplishment, we grow until it is no longer impossible for us.

An unstructured meditation is quite another thing. It has different purposes and is done differently. In doing it you think about a subject and simply stay with the subject and your own feelings about it. You work in a wider area than in a structured meditation and not in a precisely defined way. The subject you choose may be a word, an image, a phrase, a concept or a problem. You keep thinking about the subject you have chosen and explore your reactions and feelings about it. It differs from 'free association' (just following your inner reactions wherever they lead) in that you keep yourself to the subject itself and how you think and feel about it.

In essence there are two centre points in this type of meditation: the facts of the matter and how you feel about these facts. Thus, if you are meditating on your own capacity to love, the two centre points would be 'How do I love?' and 'How do I feel about these facts?' Your thinking is kept revolving about these two centres and folding back to them whenever it strays away. After trying the examples given in Chapter 8, a wide variety of unstructured meditations will suggest themselves.

The purpose of an unstructured meditation is primarily to loosen and free your own personality structure in a particular area (as in the ability to be aware of and to accept your own ability to love) so that you can grow in this area. If done consistently under the aid of the will to integrate oneself more fully and to grow, it does have this effect. It is not just easily musing about the subject, just drowsily wandering through it. That may be pleasant, relaxing, guided day-dreaming, but it is not meditation. The active will must be present, directing your attention more and more fully toward the subject and your relationship to it.

In the old Sufi example of the chariot, there must be a driver (a will) who knows the direction he wishes to go and is active and determined in keeping the chariot moving in that direction. The horse is the state of emotion – of a strong wish to become more than you are now, to develop. The chariot itself is the usual intellect and way of perceiving and relating to the world. All three are necessary for successful meditation of either of these two types. The driver, of course, must be in command.

There is no particular point – except experience, in seeing what it is like – in doing a meditation (either structured or unstructured) just once. For any real value it must be consistently repeated over a period of time. As you will see in Chapter 8, in which instructions for meditations are given, these periods range from a minimum of several weeks to several months or longer.

The unstructured meditation is often necessary in a meditational programme to free the emotions and feelings in special areas. Structured meditations alone may be too formal and intellectually oriented to help you move at the most rapid pace possible toward your goals. A good programme of structured meditations alone will in the long run have the desired effects, but a combination of the two seems likely to produce the fastest results. The structured meditations primarily train the intellect and will release the emotional life more slowly. In the unstructured meditations this is reversed.

A Hasidic criticism has been made of some of the results of one type of Habad Hasidism that trained mostly the will and intellect and did not do much in the way of releasing the emotional life. The criticism was that it was like turning out a good marksman who knew how to aim and fire his rifle and knew the target. The only problem was that there was no powder in his bullets. The powder here stands for the emotional freedom and thrust needed for real growth; the example is curiously similar to the Sufi analogy of the chariot needing a horse.

Another way of describing mental meditations is to classify them as meditations of the outer way, the middle way and the inner way. This classification applies to structural meditations and not in any useful manner to unstructured ones.[1]

In meditations of the outer way (also known as the way of forms), we start with something externally given, something on the outside, and work with and from that. It may be an object, a word, an image, a happening. In Chapter 8, Contemplation is a meditation of the outer way. We take an object and work at simply looking at it, exploring it actively with our eyes as one might explore a piece of velvet or a lump of alabaster by stroking it with one's hands. We try to learn to do this as nonverbally as possible, not talking in our heads about it. This meditation of the outer way is one of the hardest and (for many people) one of the most productive meditations ever devised.

Similarly, the Lotus meditation is a meditation of the outer way. In it we choose a word, image or concept and then think about it in a highly defined manner. The emphasis in the outer way is that something outside of ourselves is chosen and worked with in a special manner.

Meditations on the middle way, also known as the way of emptiness, strive toward an emptiness of the mind. Not a trance or drowsy state, what is sought for is a highly alert and dynamically balanced mind without conscious thought. When this state is reached, events are perceived and responded to as they occur with the full focus of immediate attention and with no hangups from the past or claims for the future. In the Byzantine desert Christian mystical schools (the Hesychast tradition), it is known as 'the way of the man with a silent mind'. In the Western Christian tradition there were the Quietists, who worked toward a blank state of alert passivity in order to receive His message.

I have not included any exercises of this middle way in this book. It is a long, hard way, producing results only after a long period of time. Further, it includes some traps (see page 72) that take the help of a good teacher to avoid. Unless you are willing to make the long commitment necessary and have a teacher highly skilled in this approach (there are a few such Zen teachers available in the United States), it is probably just as well to let the middle way go.

Meditations of the inner way, also known as the way of expression or the way of surrender, start with what is going on in your own inner life; you respond to this in special ways. In the Bubble meditation of Chapter 8, you observe your own thoughts, perceptions and reactions in a special slowly timed manner, observing each one for about the same period of time. You do not try to *do* anything with these, or deliberately follow them in any way, just observe them. The inner way consists of meditations on your own stream of consciousness.

Many meditations are combinations of these classes and hard to define beyond this. The Theraveda meditation in Chapter 8, in which you concentrate on one of your own internally generated rhythms (as on the rise and fall of your abdomen during breathing), is a combination meditation, although technically speaking it is probably a meditation of the outer way. It seems to fall somewhere between the inner and outer ways, however.

Although all three ways, if followed and worked with consistently, lead to the same places, each has its own special effects and emphases along the road. The outer way tends to bring, during the work, special strength to one's feeling of competence and the ability to cope with the world. Confidence in the self and the resultant ability to make decisions quickly and accurately are increased.

The middle way brings a special strength to one's ability to remain calm and 'unflappable' in the face of outside events. Among other things it reduces your claims on how things 'should be' and therefore your response to them is less filled with irrelevant emotions.

The inner way especially increases your awareness and acceptance of your own emotional life, your feelings. It becomes easier to enjoy and express them. Thus, if this is a particular problem at this stage of your development, you might well choose to emphasize meditations of the inner way in your meditational programme.

7

MYSTICISM, MEDITATION AND THE PARANORMAL

In the long history of mysticism there are constant reports of paranormal occurrences. Again and again we read the descriptions of mystics acquiring information through telepathy, clairvoyance and precognition. Not only are there frequent reports of this kind, there are also a great many warnings in documents on mystical training that the student should not pay too much attention to these occurrences, as they are likely to sidetrack him from the main task of growing and developing himself. It appears unlikely that these warnings would be repeated so often – and in almost identical terms in writings from schools that had little or no communication with each other – if there were not the possibility of these occurrences actually happening.

The differentiation between telepathy and clairvoyance and precognition is probably an artificial one. If a person demonstrates that he has knowledge that he could not have acquired by means of his senses nor figured out from previously known information, we call it 'telepathy' if it is known to anyone else at that time, 'clairvoyance' if it is not. If the information concerns events that will happen in the future, we call it 'precognition'. In all probability these terms refer to the same process of gathering information. It is for this reason that J. B. Rhine coined the term 'Extra Sensory Perception' (ESP) to cover all these events.

Are there really events that can be validly classified as examples of Extra Sensory Perception, of knowledge gained outside of the usual ways? It is the common belief in our culture that there cannot be, that such an idea is so obviously opposed to common sense that it must be untrue.[1] There is much truth in this view. In the world as we know it these things cannot happen; one gains knowledge by the senses or by thinking through the implications of knowledge one has already gained by the senses. There is no other way.

The problem is that these events do occur. 'Paranormal' is the common word for them. The science that studies them is called 'Parapsychology' or 'Psychical Research'. The evidence is there, hard and definitive, for anyone who wishes to look at it. This includes not only carefully studied reports of spontaneous cases – cases that just 'happened' – but also precisely planned laboratory studies done with the most careful methods of modern scientific procedure.[2] We are faced with a real and upsetting paradox: What cannot happen clearly does!

One way past this paradox concerns altered states of consciousness. In an altered state of consciousness, you view the world as if it were put together in a different fashion than the way you usually view it. This by no means implies that you are insane or deluding yourself. Einsteinian physics is a statement that the world is put together and 'works' in a different way than is believed in a commonsense view or by the older, 'classical' physics. No one would call an Einsteinian physicist insane because of his views. The physicist would say he was using 'a different metaphysical system', a different explanation of reality. The mystic would say he was in 'an altered state of consciousness.' The only difference between the two is that the physicist is describing, analysing intellectually, and examining the implications of this other view of reality; the mystic is perceiving and reacting to it. The first is talking about something, the second is living in it.

One of the interesting things about different metaphysical systems is that, very often, what is impossible in one system is possible in another. In each of them certain events are permissible, certain events are not permissible. As I have described in the previous chapters, one of the goals of meditation is to shift oneself to a specific different state of consciousness, to the *use* of a specific different metaphysical system. In the system one shifts to, Extra Sensory Perception is permissible and 'normal'. It often does occur.[3]

The answer to the paradox of events happening that cannot happen thus becomes clearer. It cannot happen in our usual state of consciousness, when we are using our everyday system of describing and explaining reality. It can happen when we are in a different state of consciousness, using a different system of describing and explaining reality.

It is likely, whether one accepts the above theory or not, that para-normal events will occur as one seriously gets into the work of medi-tation. (If we are training, among other things, to go into an altered state of consciousness in which ESP is 'normal', we should not be too surprised if examples of it occur.) The question is not really whether or not these strange acquisitions of knowledge sometimes occur; the question is what to do about them if they do occur.

Many people, when these events happen, get so interested in them and excited about their occurrence that they lose all their orienta-tion to the real goals of meditation. They become more concerned with the paranormal than with their own development. And, with this point of view, that their meditation is for the purpose of producing strange and fascinating events ('siddhis', as the Buddhists call them), their meditation ceases to help them develop themselves. Frequently they then begin to base their own estimate of their worth on the paranormal phenomena they produce. It becomes their *raison d'être*, the reason they have value as a person. Unless this orientation is given up, further development is very unlikely.

Every experienced teacher of meditation knows that one of his main tasks along the way will be to make sure that his students do not get too interested in these phenomena. In the seminars I have conducted, we regard the telepathic occurrences that begin to happen pretty regularly when the group has worked together for a few days with an attitude of 'that's nice; now let's get back to serious matters.'

The ESP occurrences that often happen during meditation have led many people to a serious interest in parapsychology. This, of course, is an entirely different matter.

One thing may make it easier for some people to accept this knowledge without anxiety. This is the fact that there is not a single good example in the entire scientific literature of someone gaining information 'paranormally' (by ESP) when the person who originally held the information really wished to keep it secret. We do not receive telepathic knowledge if the person who has it really does not want us to know of it.

The only type of reaction to ESP events during a programme of meditation that makes any sense is to pretty much ignore them. Certainly it is reasonable to regard them as 'interesting' and as sort of pleasantly irridescent bubbles that add to the colour of the world, but not to place much importance on them. In a practical, realistic sense they are *not* important. We must base our plans and actions on the far more reliable information we get from our senses and from the analysis of information we acquire by means of our senses. Planning and acting on the basis of paranormally acquired information is just plain kookiness at this stage of our knowledge of the paranormal.

This is a viewpoint I learned from Eileen Garrett, who was probably the most talented and most widely and carefully studied acquirer of paranormal information of our time. (The technical term for a person with a great deal of ability in this area is a 'sensitive'.) Mrs Garrett believed that one *never* acted on the basis of information acquired through paranormal means, only on the information acquired by normal means. She made one exception to this rule. If you have never had any particularly strong fear of flying and are about to get on an aeroplane and feel a very strong, unusual anxiety about going on this particular plane, delay your flight to a later one. This response was the only exception to her rule.

In addition, if you allow yourself to be drawn into too much interest and concern with ESP occurrences during meditational practices, they will be used by those parts of your being that do not want to accept the self-discipline you are trying to learn. For a while you will produce more and more Extra Sensory Perception, the value of your meditations to you will cease, then the paranormal occurrences will stop and you will be left where you were before you started except that your work in mediation has stalled. The trap is seductive and easy to fall into and must be avoided.

Of course these phenomena are interesting and exciting, but if one becomes preoccupied with them focus on meditation is soon lost. It is important to keep this danger in mind and to avoid the temptation to be side-tracked by these fascinating phenomena.

THE 'HOW' OF MEDITATION

≈

In this chapter I will give instructions for a number of meditations. These will include examples of all major types (except an example of a meditation of the middle way).[1] The instructions will be detailed enough so that, by reading them over a few times before meditating and then reading them over again after each of the first few times you practise, you should be able to learn how to meditate in these ways.

Do not expect to do a meditation 'well' (focusing on it and nothing else) for a long period of time. The first major effect of meditation, strengthening the personality structure, comes from working consistently on it, not on doing it 'well'. The important thing about a meditation is how hard and consistently you work on it, not how well you do it. This point *cannot* be overstated. It is a crucial truth, but most people simply do not believe it. Only after a long period of practice can you expect to be really just doing a meditation and not anything else. Saint Bernard of Clairvaux (who had certainly worked long and hard on his meditations) was once asked how much, when he was meditating, he was really 'into it,' really just doing it. He replied with a sigh that still echoes down the centuries, 'Oh how rare the hour and how brief its duration!'

A story about Saint Teresa of Avila illustrates the same point. One of her novices remarked that it must be wonderful to be like Teresa and not be bothered by distractions in her prayers and meditations. Saint Teresa replied, 'What do you think I am, a saint?'

It is only after you have worked a long time and reaped the benefit of the first part of the path in its personality strengthening, increased ability to relate to and cope with the world, ability to accept and express your own feelings, etc., that the second effect – helping you to attain a new way of being in the world, a new metaphysical system – emerges.[2] The road is long and often frustrating, but the game is worth the candle. Let us fare on.

Start by finding a comfortable position in a quiet time and place. If the place feels good to you (has 'good vibes'), that is nice too; it is not essential, but helpful.

THE MEDITATION OF CONTEMPLATION

This meditation – called in Eastern schools 'One-pointing' – is used by a wide variety of mystical schools. Essentially it is learning to look at something actively, dynamically, alertly, but without words. You pick an object to work with (generally speaking, it is best for most people to start with a natural object, a bit of seashell, a pebble, a twig) and look at it with the same structure as if you were feeling it, as if you were using your sense of touch to stroke a piece of velvet.

Let me try to make this clearer. Take a part of your sleeve or the cloth covering your thigh. Stroke it with your hand, 'feel' it. Do this for half a minute or a minute. Then look at it for the same amount of time. Really *look* at it, learn it by eye. For most people there is a real difference between the two perceptions. With the visual sense, you tend to use words to describe the sensation, to translate the experience into language. With the tactile sense, you tend to accept the experience on a nonverbal level.

Contemplation is a structured meditation of the outer way. You take the object, hold it at a comfortable eye range for you, feeling free to move it closer or farther away as you please, and just *look* at it.

It is very hard. Give yourself permission to make constant slips from the directions. You will make them anyway and will be much more comfortable – and get along better with this exercise – if you give yourself permission in advance. Treat yourself as if you were a much-loved child that an adult was trying to keep walking on a narrow sidewalk. The child is full of energy and keeps running off to the fields on each side to pick flowers, feel the grass, climb a tree. Each time you are aware of the child leaving the path, you say in effect, 'Oh, that's how children are. Okay, honey, back to the sidewalk,' and bring yourself gently but firmly and alertly back to just looking. Again and again you will suddenly notice that you are thinking about something else or translating your perception into words or something of the sort. Each time, you should say the equivalent, 'Oh, that's where I am now; back to work,' and come back to looking.

A man came to the Zen master Ikkyo and asked him for some words of wisdom to guide him in life. Ikkyo nodded agreeably and wrote on a piece of paper the word 'attention.' The man said he could not understand and asked for something more. Ikkyo wrote 'attention, attention.' After a further request for an explanation, Ikkyo wrote his final statement for the man. 'Attention, attention, attention means attention.'

In training her students in this technique, Saint Teresa of Avila wrote, 'I do not require of you to form great and serious considerations in your thinking. I require of you only to look.' A Byzantine mystic, Nicophorus the Solitary, put it, 'Attention is the appeal of the soul to itself.' The Baal Shem Tov wrote, 'God's miracles belong to those who can concentrate on one thing and limit themselves.' And a statement attributed to the Buddha runs in part, 'In what is seen should be only the seen.'

Rabbi Dov Baer, one of the great teachers of mysticism in the Hasidic school, wrote: 'I will teach you the best way to say Torah. You must be nothing but an ear which hears what the universe of the word is saying in you. The moment you hear what you yourself are saying, you must stop.'

Patanjali, an Eastern sage, called this technique 'fixed attention' and described it as 'binding the mind staff to a place.' We must, however, bind ourselves gently and with humour and compassion at our own lack of discipline.

This lack of trained discipline of our own will becomes immediately apparent as we do this exercise. In the words of one student of it, we find ourselves 'itching, twitching and bitching.' We find ourselves constantly needing to change our physical position, or getting sleepy, or using words to describe our perception, or suddenly solving problems we have been concerned with for weeks, or unable to concentrate, or anything else we can dream up to avoid the discipline. Or we notice that for a moment we were 'just looking' and begin to think about how well we are doing at the meditation and, thereby, of course, stray right off the track. (This has been called The Law of the Good Moment, otherwise known as 'Here I am, wasn't I!')

One way we frequently avoid discipline is by the production of what the Zen people call 'Makyo'. Makyo are illusions that we project on reality as an aid to escaping from the directions. Your seashell or pebble may develop a pretty corona of coloured light or apparently begin to accordion in size, growing larger and smaller. You may feel yourself grow lighter or heavier or feel as if currents of rather pleasant energy are running through you. Every sort of sensation from smells to touches to sounds to lights is possible. The Suringama Sutra (a mystical training document of ancient India) lists fifty types of Makyo and then goes on to explain that these are only the most typical types. The best way to respond to these is to say to yourself, in effect, 'Oh, that's what I'm perceiving now. How interesting. I wonder what I will make up next to avoid the discipline. Now, back to just looking.' Yasutani Roshi, an experienced Zen teacher, said of these, 'Makyo do not occur when you are dawdling, neither do they appear when your practice has ripened . . . They indicate the intensity of your concentration.' He goes on to warn you to be careful not to get too interested or involved with them as they prevent progress if you do.[3]

Saint Gregory of Sinai, in his meditational training manual *Instructions to Hesychasts*, wrote, 'When, while you work, you see within or without you a light or a flame or an image – of Christ, for example, or of an angel, or of someone else – do not accept it lest you suffer harm. And do not yourself create fantasies nor pay attention to those that create themselves.'⁴

The task is to look actively and alertly. You must keep trying to bring more and more of yourself to just doing this one thing – looking. You are aiming at being totally involved, from your head to your toes, in this intense, nonverbal activity, to be as totally involved as is a dog pointing at a rabbit. In the words of the Bhagavad-Gita, 'to hold the senses and imagination in check and to keep the mind concentrated upon its object.'

Hold the object you have chosen at a comfortable visual distance from you and be flexible about this distance. Do not stare at one point on the object. Dynamically explore it without words. Treat it as a fascinating new continent you are exploring nonverbally. If you stare or strain your eyes during the exercise you will simply increase the illusions (eye fatigue plus Makyo) and slow yourself down. Contemplation is 'binding the mind staff to a place.' It is *not* binding the retina to a place.

Stay, if at all possible, with the same object for several weeks (at least) at a time. A nature object is often best, but do not choose a flower. A flower as a contemplation object is, for many people, too easy and we tend to slip into dazed, trance-like states with it. There are also some objects that, because of the symbolic, unconscious and archetypal meanings, are quite difficult and should not be used until you are thoroughly experienced with this exercise. (This means a minimum of several months of daily work.) These difficult objects include a cross, a fire, a mandala. Save these until much later or your work will probably be greatly slowed.

In my own training seminars I have participants use a paper match. (Christmas Humphreys uses brass doorknobs.) These are generally fine when working with the aid of the discipline of an intensive group. However, if working alone, they are frequently just too dull and dispiriting; nature objects are better or, if you feel good about it, a small, fairly plain piece of personal jewellery.

Staying with the same object tends to make the exercise go better. Work for ten-minute periods for the first two weeks on a daily basis.

If your schedule makes this impossible, work at least five times a week. After two or three weeks, increase the time to fifteen minutes and a month later to twenty minutes. After a month of this you will know where you stand with this meditation and may want to increase it to one-half-hour, or you may feel twenty minutes are right for you. Or that you wish to leave it out of your meditational programme.

Expect it to be different each time. The fact that it goes 'well' one period makes no prediction for the next. There will be 'good' sessions and frustrating, discouraging ones. About all you can predict as you go on is a tendency to go to more and more extremes and that when they are good they are very good and when not good, intensely frustrating. This is a tough but excellent meditation and, in the words of Richard Rolle, the beautiful thirteenth-century British mystic, 'Contemplative sweetness not without full great labour is gotten.'

THE MEDITATION OF BREATH COUNTING

There is a very wide variety of meditations utilizing your own breathing. The particular one described here is, with a minor modification, used particularly in Zen training.

In this structured meditation of the outer way, the object again is to be doing just one thing as completely and fully as possible. In this case the one thing is counting the exhalations of your breath, your breathing out. You strive to be aware of just counting and to be as fully aware of it as possible. All your attention is gently and firmly and repeatedly brought to bear on this activity. The goal is to have your whole being involved in the counting. Saint Anthony the Great described something of the goal you are working toward when he wrote, 'The prayer of the monk is not perfect until he no longer realizes himself or the fact that he is praying.'

In this exercise one is paying as full and complete attention as possible to the counting itself. Thoughts, feelings, impressions, sensory perceptions, to the degree that they are conscious, are a wandering away from the instructions. In the words of the Bhagavad-Gita, 'The tortoise can draw in his legs/The seer can draw in his senses.' It is this 'drawing in of the senses' you are working toward in this discipline.

It is probably best for most Westerners to count up to four and repeat. In Zen, the usual practice is to count up to ten. However, after working with a fairly large number of Westerners on this exercise, it seems to me that this makes the work unnecessarily difficult. Typically, when you get to seven, eight and nine in your counting you begin to worry if you will remember to change over at 'ten' and so get thrown off stride.

Another variation is to count sequentially as high as you go during each session. The problem here is that it is very difficult to avoid self-competition, the sort of inner statement that goes, 'Yesterday I counted up to 947. Will I go higher today?' All in all, a count of four seems like the best available compromise.

When you find yourself thinking about your counting (or about anything else), you are wandering away from the instructions and you should bring yourself gently back. If you find yourself modifying your breathing, this also is a straying from the exercise.

One permissible variation on the exercise as given here is to include an 'and' between the counts to 'fill up' the space between exhalations. This makes it easier for some people. Thus you would count 'one' for the first exhalation, 'and' for the next inhalation, 'two' for the second exhalation, 'and' for the next inhalation, and so forth. After trying it for a few sessions with just the 'one, two, three, four' try it for a session with the 'and' included and then make your own decision. As in all meditations, it is essential before you start a session to decide exactly what it is to consist of and then stick to it.

Be comfortable and set a timer or put a clock-face where it is in your line of vision. For most people this exercise goes better with the eyes closed since there is less distraction. Experiment and see whether it is better for you with your eyes opened or closed. If closed you will have to 'peek' once in a while to see how your time is going. Start with fifteen minutes at a time on a daily, or else a five times a week, basis if necessary. After a few weeks, increase to twenty minutes, and after another month to twenty-five or thirty minutes. After working this last schedule for a month or two, you should be able to determine your own future course with this meditation.

THE MEDITATION OF THE BUBBLE

This is a structured meditation of the inner way. In meditations of this sort, you observe your own consciousness in a special way (through the structured design of the meditation) while interfering with it as little as possible. You meditate on the stream of your own consciousness.

Picture yourself sitting quietly and comfortably on the bottom of a clear lake. You know how slowly large bubbles rise through the water. Each thought, feeling, perception, etc., is pictured as a bubble rising into the space you can observe, passing through and out of this space. It takes five to seven or eight seconds to complete this process. When you have a thought or feeling, you simply observe it for this time period until it passes out of your visual space. Then you wait for the next one and observe it for the same amount of time, and so on. You do not explore, follow up or associate to a bubble, just observe it with the background of 'Oh, that's what I'm thinking (or feeling or sensing) now. How interesting.' Then, as it passes out of visual space (as the imaginary bubble rises), you calmly wait for the next bubble.

Do not be thrown off the meditation if the same 'bubble' rises several times. If you just go on, this will pass. And do not be disturbed if you cannot see the connection between the bubbles or the source of your thoughts. If you simply stay with the discipline long enough, most confusing connections will clear up. If your mind seems to go 'blank', why, feeling 'blank' makes a fine bubble!

The purpose of the concept of bubbles rising through the water is to help you do two things. The first is to keep the timing. You learn to simply contemplate each thought or perception for (approximately) a definite time and then to let it go. Secondly, the structure helps you look at each one individually and not constantly feel you must find connections between them. Since these are crucial reasons for this structure, those who find the idea of sitting at the bottom of a lake unsympathetic or disturbing can picture themselves on a warm, windless day on the prairie watching large, separate puffs of smoke rise from a camp-fire as if it were an Indian signal fire.

Another variation of this is the Tibetan 'thoughts are logs' discipline. In this you picture yourself sitting on the bank of a broad, gentle river. From time to time logs come floating down the river; you follow the same procedure, using the logs concept instead of the bubble concept. This approach is preferable for some people while others find it extremely difficult and confusing. The structure and purpose of the two ways of bubbles and logs are the same. For most people the bubble concept seems to go better.

Start with ten minutes a day for two weeks. If you are having special difficulties, on the fourth to seventh day experiment for a session with either the 'puffs of smoke' or the 'thoughts are logs' conceptualization. Try both of them if you wish, one session for each. After that choose one of the conceptualizations and stay with it. After the two weeks of ten minutes each, go to twenty minutes a day (one-half hour if this is clearly a 'right' meditation for you at this period in your development) for three weeks to a month. At the end of that time you should know how to include this meditation in your own programme.

A MEDITATION OF THE THERAVEDA TYPE

The Theraveda school of meditation is one of the few surviving sects of Hinyana Buddhism (see Chapter 9). Meditations of its approach frequently are concerned with contemplation of self-generated rhythms. You choose a body rhythm that you automatically produce and contemplate ('one-point') it. The goal again is to be doing just one thing at a time. This contemplation is again (as in the discipline of contemplation described on page 47) a nonverbal, active, alert exploration.

Find a comfortable position with your hands resting on your chest or abdomen. Many people find that this is best done lying flat on the floor, but sitting in a comfortable chair is completely acceptable. Spread your fingers so that they are not touching each other and your hands are separated. Feel what is going on immediately under your fingers. Observe actively, explore with vigour. When you find yourself translating the experience into words, you are not following the discipline and you must bring yourself back to it. Do the same if you find yourself modifying your breathing rhythm or speculating on what is going on inside your abdomen. Essentially follow the directions of the first meditation, but contemplate with your finger-tips instead of your eyes and on the rhythm of movement rather than on a natural object.

Start with fifteen minutes at a time for two weeks. At the end of that time either discard the meditation as not being right for you or else go to twenty or twenty-five minutes for another three or four weeks. At the end of that time decide for yourself how, if at all, to use this meditation in your own programme.

Other self-generated rhythms are also used by the Theraveda school. One of the most useful for many people is to contemplate what is occurring at the entrance to the nose where the air enters and leaves the body. (Eastern mystics generally feel it is important to breathe through the nostrils rather than the mouth. This may be a comment on the dust typically in the air in India or they may have a different and more widely applicable reason. I just do not know.) In this meditation one simply (it is by no means simple; it is as hard as any other meditation) contemplates what is perceived (your sensations) at this area. The same rules as in the meditations of Contemplation and Breath Counting are followed.

One self-generated rhythm that has been used by some people is the pulse-rate. This is observed either in the moving of an artery or the artery is palpated. I strongly recommend *not* doing this without the constant supervision of an experienced and medically trained teacher. It is very difficult in this one to avoid modifying your own pulse-rate, and anyone who plays around with his own heartbeat in this fashion needs either a good psychiatrist or a certificate of entry into the nearest home for the feebleminded.

THE MEDITATION OF THE THOUSAND-PETALED LOTUS

The symbol of the lotus with the thousand petals is widely used in Eastern mysticism. It is a symbolic rendition of the idea that everything is connected to everything else and that nothing is really separate and isolated from all the rest of the universe. The centre of the lotus is any object or event you may choose. Each of the petals symbolizes the connection between the centre and something else. The idea of a 'thousand' petals is symbolic of an infinity of them: there is no limit to the number of petals in this concept.

This is a structured meditation of the outer way. A word, idea, image is chosen by you to be the centre of the lotus for this exercise. I strongly recommend that for the first ten to fifteen times you use this meditation you choose words with good feelings for you, words like 'flower', 'love', 'peace', 'light', 'colour', 'grass', 'tree', 'home', etc. Unless you have had at least this much practice with this meditation, words with unpleasant feelings (i.e., 'angry', 'cry', 'sad', 'hurt', 'pain', etc.) are very likely to have you finish the meditation feeling a lot worse than you did when you started. You are likely to wind up quite depressed and possibly anxious. Words like 'empty', 'void', and 'nothingness' should not be used until after at least twenty to twenty-five sessions with this discipline. Unless you are some kind of a nut who likes depressions or bad trips, stay away from this type of word until you have had this much experience (preferably more) with this exercise. When you have practised sufficiently with this meditation, any word, image or concept may be used for its centre. In Walt Whitman's words, 'And there is no object so soft but it makes a hub for the wheeled universe.'

Once you have chosen the centre word, get comfortable, contemplate it and wait. Presently your first association to it comes to you. You look at the two words connected by the first 'petal path' and regard them for three to four seconds. You either understand the reason for the association or you do not. In either case you do nothing more than regard the centre, the path and the association for the three to four seconds. Then you return to the centre word and wait for the next association and repeat the procedure, and so forth. This is *not* free association; you always return to the word you have designated as the centre of the lotus and proceed again from there.

I will illustrate this meditation with a short series of associations. I choose the word 'light' as the centre. My first association is 'sun'. I regard the two, 'light' and 'sun', and the petal path between them for three or four seconds. I understand the connection. I return to 'light'. The next association is 'red'. I look at this for three to four seconds. I understand the connection and return to 'light'. The next association is 'dark'. I understand it and, after three to four seconds, return to 'light'. The next association is 'heavy'. I understand this and return after the time period to 'light'. The next association is 'umbrella'. I do not understand this. After three to four seconds I return to 'light'. The next association is 'bulb'. I understand it and return after three to four seconds to 'light', and so forth.

Sometimes I may run into clusters of associations. For example, 'red' could have been followed by 'blue', then by 'green', etc. If this happens, simply stay with the discipline even if it means going around the spectrum several times. Presently it will cease. If you run into a series of associations you do not understand, there is a very good chance that if you stay with it they will clear up. For example, in the series given above, the association 'umbrella' later reappeared in conjunction with 'roof', 'blindfold', 'stupidity' and some others generally belonging to the class of things that shut out 'light'.

This meditation, like the bubble meditation, often leads to surprising insights about your inner life if consistently worked with. These are good and generally useful when they happen, but must not be regarded as the main purpose of the discipline. There is an exception to this that is valid after you have had some experience with this meditation. After you have done it at least ten to fifteen times, it can be useful sometimes to solve particular problems. If I find myself in conflict with Bob and do not seem able to resolve it, I mights use the word 'conflict' or 'Bob' as the centre of the lotus. Then I proceed with the discipline in the ordinary way with no special expectations. Sometimes this leads to helpful insights. However, I strongly recommend not using this meditation as a way of solving problems until you are experienced with it.

Start with ten minutes a day for two weeks. Then go to twenty minutes or a half hour a day for three weeks to a month. At the end of that time you should know how best to include (or not) this meditation in your own programme.

THE MANTRA MEDITATION

The Mantra is one of the most widely used forms of meditation. We find it in every major mystical training school, with the possible exception of Hasidism. It consists of a word or phrase or sentence chanted over and over and over again. The basic goal is to be doing one thing at a time, in this case chanting and being aware of your chanting and only of your chanting. Whether one chants the Eastern 'Hare Krishna,' or 'Aum,' the Christian 'Deus in adjutorium meum intende' ('Oh God, come to my aid'), the Sufi 'Allah hu' or any other sounds, the basic goal remains the same.

It is necessary to say that two other reasons are given for the value of mantras by various mystical training schools. Although I personally do not agree that these reasons are valid, the contrary opinion is held by many men who are very serious students of the subject and whose viewpoints must be treated with respect.

The first set of reasons concerns the *content* of the mantra. Many meditators believe that a specific content has real value in helping you comprehend and *know* its validity. Thus the chant 'All is One', if repeated enough, will from this viewpoint, bring you closer to the knowledge that this is true. Similarly, chants such as 'God is One' or 'God is good' are believed to have beneficial effects because of their content.

The second set of reasons given for the positive value of mantras is beleived by some to be in the 'vibrational' qualities of certain sounds and the effect of these vibrations on specific parts of the body or personality. Thus certain sounds are supposed to vibrate chiefly in certain organs of the body and to thereby stimulate these organs into greater effectiveness and/or to bring them into a better relationship with other organs and personality areas. This type of explanation is found chiefly in the Yoga and Sufi schools. Although I must confess that I cannot understand exactly what they are talking about, these claims are made by men of such seriousness and experience that they cannot be taken lightly.

However, anybody who gives (or sells) you a mantra designed just for you on the basis of ten minutes' conversation is pulling your leg. The mantra will probably work but certainly not because it is designed for you, but because you use it as a mantra.

A short phrase is chosen. I prefer meaningless phrases since I believe that the meaning of the content makes it harder to stay with the structure, but if you feel fairly strongly that a phrase with positive content would be more sympathetic, use one of these. I have known people to usefully work with mantras such as 'Love one another', 'Peace', 'Peace to all', etc. The classic Eastern and Christian phrases just mentioned have also been useful to many. One man I know of used Thoreau's phrase 'I have heard no bad news' effectively, although this is a bit long. '*Kyrie eleison*' ('Lord have mercy') and 'Alleluia' have also been used. Saint Gregory of Sinai recommends, 'I am the way, the truth and the light.' One mystical training school believes all mantras should be seven syllables in length, but I do not understand their reasoning.

One of the nonsense phrases I have used with groups is 'La-de' ('Lah-dee'). This mantra was designed by means of LeShan's Telephone Book Method, which is probably as effective as any other. Open a telephone book at random and put a finger down blindly.

Take the first syllable of the name you hit. Repeat the procedure. Link the two syllables and you have a mantra.

Find a comfortable position but do not slouch in such a way as to constrict your chest and throat. Start chanting the phrase. Do this aloud if possible, but if not, do it without making actual sounds. It's best to do it audibly but not too loudly or you will strain your voice, or even hyperventilate (breathe more rapidly and deeply than your oxygen needs require) and so alter the chemical environment of your brain. This can make you dizzy and produces other symptoms sometimes. It is generally a pretty silly thing to do.

Keep trying to chant and nothing else. Keep bringing yourself back to the task and trying to involve yourself more and more in it. Find one rhythm that seems sympathetic to yourself and the phrase. Stay with that rhythm. Stay with it through all the silliness you will dream up, seeing new meanings in the phrase, punning on it, finding its meaning break down into nonsense (if it isn't nonsense already), and God knows what else. Your task is to follow the discipline and to keep working at doing nothing else but chanting and being aware of your chanting. If a mantra is right for you at this stage of your development, after five to eight sessions you will find increasingly periods of time (five seconds or up to twenty) when you are only aware of your chanting.

Start with fifteen minutes at a time. Then, after two weeks, increase this to twenty minutes (or a half hour if you feel really good about this discipline) and keep this up for another two or three weeks. Then decide if, and if so, how, you wish to integrate this form of meditation into your own meditational programme.

THE MEDITATION OF 'WHO AM I?'

In Chapter 3, I discussed the fact that it is impossible, with our usual ways of perceiving and thinking, to find the *individuality* of something, the way it differs completely and inescapably from all other things. We can only find qualities it has or does not have and to what degree it has them. As long as we stay at this level of conceptualization, it is always possible to imagine another thing with the same percentages of the same qualities, and therefore, by our standards of reason, identical with the first, even though we *know* it is not identical. It is only by the use of another way of perceiving and comprehending the world that we can really understand what our inner knowledge tells us is certainly true: that each of us is truly individual and unique. We must force into existence this new way of being in the world if we wish to solve the paradox. Conversely, by attempting to solve this paradox we can aid this new way of being to come to conscious existence.

It is not surprising, therefore, that a meditation based on this paradox has been used, in one variation or another, in a number of mystical training schools. Ramana Maharshi calls it 'self-enquiry' and terms it 'the direct method'. In the Christian tradition we find it introduced by Meister Eckhart.

This is an exceptionally rigorous and difficult meditation. Until you have had several months of daily practice at the very least, with structured meditations you simply are not ready to do it. It is a structured meditation of the inner way and can, for some people, be an exceptionally rich and productive discipline.

In this meditation we ask the question 'Who am I?' and respond to each answer we find in a highly structured manner. If a name seems to be the answer, we (inwardly) reply, 'No, that is a name I have given myself. Who is the I who I gave that name to?' If it is felt or perceived, as in 'I am the person who feels tired,' the reply is 'No, that is a sensation I feel. Who is the I who has that sensation?' If it is a memory, as in 'I am the person who once . . . ,' the reply is 'No, that is a memory I have. Who is the I that has that memory?' If it is an image or picture of yourself, the reply is 'No, that is an image I have of myself. Who is the I that has this image?' If a monster or an angel seems to be an answer, the reply is 'No, that is an interpretation of memory and idea I have. Who is the I who has the interpretation?' All answers that arise to the question are responded to in this way. After each response there is an active, dynamic search for the next answer.

There is no rest in this meditation. It must be done with a kind of continued fierceness that constantly states the rejection of the previous answer and searches for the next answer in order to reject and go past it. The *structure* of this meditation must be carefully followed in exact detail. Each statement is made in the same way and in the present tense.

The Buddhist version of this meditation is the '*Neti, Neti*' ('Not this, not that') meditation. The version given here is closer to Eckhart's who writes:

What the soul does, it does through agents. It understands by means of intelligence. If it remembers, it does so by means of memory. If it is to love, the will must be used and thus it acts always through agents and not within its own essence (Sermon 1).

... if you are to experience this noble birth, you must depart from all crowds and go back to the starting point, the core out of which you came. The crowds are the agents of the soul and their activities: memory, understanding, will, in all their diversifications. You must leave them all: sense perception, imagination, and all that you discover in self or intend to do (Sermon 4).

The Svetatavatara Upanishad puts it, 'Meditate on the light in the centre of the fire – meditate, that is, upon pure consciousness as distinct from the ordinary consciousness of the intellect.'

In the Eastern sense, this is the direct search for the Atman, the real essence of the self that lies behind the many false selves with which we ordinarily identify ourselves.

When you are ready for this meditation, do it for a half hour at a time each day for one to two weeks. At that time you will know if it is one you should continue and, if so, how to pace your own work.

Sometimes in doing it you will find an answer for yourself that is the answer for this particular session of work. When you have found this answer (you will know it when you do), stop the session there and just sit quietly with it for a while. When you have found the final

answer for you (for this particular period in your life) from this meditation, you will also know it and stop working with this meditation
at that point.

A Sufi Movement Meditation

This meditation requires a group of from five to fifteen people. It is a
meditation of movement and chanting and is described here in order
to introduce and give the flavour of this type of meditation work.

In movement meditations, as in the other forms I have described,
the primary goal is to learn to do, at will, one thing at a time. In addition, movement meditations are the best overall route for some
people and are an exceedingly valuable variation and change of pace
in a meditational programme for many others. I strongly recommend that somewhere in your own programme you try either this
meditation or the next one, a meditation of the sensory awareness
(Elsa Gindler) method. The change to the route of physical movement also releases the whole organism you are and makes it more
coherent and integrated by including the body instead of leaving it
out. There is, to my knowledge, no serious mystical training school
that does not include some movement work, and this, in itself,
should tell us something.

In this meditation you and your companions form a circle with
hands clasped. Leave some distance between each of you, but not so
much that you are stretching your arms. Place your feet comfortably apart so that you are solidly set on the earth. Slowly lean back-
ward, raise your face to the sky and your hands upward, and when
looking as straight up as is comfortable say in a ringing voice, 'Ya
Hai'. Bring the body and head forward and the arms down and back
until you are facing as directly downward as is comfortable. Say in
the same voice 'Ya Huk'. Now move upward to the 'Ya Hai' position
and repeat. Move together until you find a group speed and rhythm
that feel right. Many groups do this at between ten and fourteen
pairs per minute, but find your group's own best pace. The 'Ya Hai' is

a ringing, upward, triumphant call. The 'Ya Huk' has the same qualities, but its abrupt ending produces a different feeling. Once you have found the pace, keep at it. Your goal is total involvement of your awareness in the movement and chant. When going well the group should be opening and closing like a flower.

You must be aware of the physical condition of each person in this. If anyone feels he is pushing himself where he should not be, he steps back, brings together the hands of the persons on each side of him and leaves the circle intact as he withdraws. Everyone must feel free to do this or it is a mistake to do this exercise.

Practice it for ten to fifteen minutes about ten times until you really begin to feel the group getting into it and that no one is uncomfortable or strained by the exercise. If it goes well, begin to increase it to a half hour. The goal is to be able to go past the fatigue point to where you are moving and chanting so completely and so unaware of anything else that fatigue drops away and the only awareness of the self and the universe is the total harmony and action of movement and sound. If this exercise is right for you, you will find this way of being and notice afterward that you were so completely integrated and doing only one thing so completely that you were hardly tired at all once you had gone past the first fatigue, got your 'second wind'. Once you have reached this place a few times you will be able to decide whether and (if so) how to included this exercise in your meditational programme.

A SENSORY AWARENESS MEDITATION

The following meditation is also a movement meditation, but of a different sort than the Sufi dance. It comes from the sensory awareness approach started by Elsa Gindler. The following instructions were written by Dorothy Friedman, an experienced and expert teacher of this method.

Just as breathing frequently plays a central role in various schools of meditation, so it is an underlying theme in using your body as a focus for meditation. It is important in the sequences that follow that breathing remains in the fore-front of consciousness, along with awareness of the particular part of the body you are concentrating upon.

The first essential task is to make your body as comfortable as possible. Begin by lying flat on the floor on your back, preferably on a rug or on some type of mat to soften the ground surface slightly. Either allow your legs to be fully extended, or, if this creates discomfort in your lower back, bend your knees, allowing your feet to stand close to your buttocks. Close your eyes and concentrate for some minutes on letting each part of your body settle more deeply into the floor. Begin with your feet and continue on to the calves, knees, thighs, pelvis (abdomen), rib cage, chest, hands, lower arms, elbows, upper arms, neck, and finally head. Try to be aware that in all these parts you are three-dimensional. Be conscious of the top side as well as the side that touches the floor, and the side-to-side areas as well. Now just concentrate on your breath as you exhale. Feel your whole body sinking more deeply into the floor.

This period of concentration should precede any further meditational practices. If you really allow a full ten to twenty minutes for it, you will find that you have increased your receptivity and inner quiet to a great degree. It will also help to unravel the kinks and inner tensions in muscles that are deeply layered and below ordinary awareness.

If you have time and wish to continue further along these lines, allow your hands to rest on your diaphragm (area between chest and waist). Begin by letting the weight of your hands really rest there, and allow them to be moved by your breathing. After a while, when your hands feel incorporated into your breathing almost as if they were mutually dependent or unified, begin very slowly to raise your hands away from your body. They need not go very high. Be sure your upper arms and elbows remain on the floor. Let the movement, as simple as it is, be as slow as possible. Try to be aware of breathing all the while. As your hands return to your diaphragm, take plenty of time to allow them to settle with all their weight. Once more allow your hands to incorporate with your breathing before you repeat the experiment. Try this many times, gradually permitting the distance your hands move from your body to increase until they eventually come to rest on the floor. Now alternate between the two resting places. The path of the movement is like a small arc opening away from your diaphragm to the floor, and from the floor to your diaphragm. After a while you may begin to feel that your breathing and your movement are so unified, you may have the sense that it all happens by itself, effortlessly. When you reach this state, you will really feel 'into it', and be aware of a deep state of relaxation and comfort.

Do not be discouraged if for some time you cannot be aware of breathing and moving simultaneously. As in other meditational practices, skill comes with time and repetition.

If you wish to try this form of meditation, either read the instructions over several times or, preferably, put them on a tape and play them to yourself on a tape recorder. If you do this, be sure to put them on slowly so they take twenty minutes to a half hour to play back. Skip plenty of time between sentences after the first paragraph. Start by doing it once a day for two weeks. At the end of that time you should know if you wish to continue it or not.

THE MEDITATION OF THE SAFE HARBOUR

This meditation is different from the previous ones presented insofar that it is almost entirely a guided 'allowing' and has much less of the 'working' aspect. The allowing, however, is carefully and constantly guided, and this nonverbal guiding process provides the discipline for this meditation. The directions here are a variation of a practice taught in the Byzantine desert (the Hesychast, or 'way of sweet repose') tradition. Exercises somewhat similar to this are also taught by some Sufi teachers.

In a comfortable position, let your consciousness drift within you.

Assume your consciousness is like a point that you can drift in any direction you wish. Assume that somewhere – within you or not – there is the safe harbour where you will feel perfectly 'at home', 'safe', 'secure', 'right', 'whole'. Assume that any verbal map to get to this place, way of being, state, is incorrect by the nature of the very fact that it is verbal. Make one more assumption. Assume that the safe harbour sends out a 'feeling', a 'signal', you can learn to sense so that you can ultimately drift yourself to it and find it.

Let yourself feel within and sense in what 'direction' you should float your consciousness. Make no assumptions as to what this direction or goal will be and try to let go of any assumptions you find yourself making. Try to talk to yourself about the process as little as possible. 'Feel' your way, sense 'signals' as to direction or dimension within you, and try to drift your consciousness accordingly without labelling the signals more than you have to, realizing that, for a long time at least, whatever labels you make will be incorrect.

It is useful for many people, although not for all, to start the drifting within their own chest area. Do not assume your final goal is or is not within this area. Try not to be verbal or intellectual about the process. It is a sensing, a putting out 'radar', rather than a process of the intellect.

The goal is a place, way of being, or whatever *you* find that is so right, so 'at home', so natural to your basic being that you feel completely safe, secure, 'right' in it. The term 'safe harbour' is used since a harbour includes these qualities but is not a place of restriction; you go out from a harbour reoriented, rested and reprovisioned as well as come into it for rest and safety.

This is a very gentle meditation. The 'effort' is less than the 'allowing'; allowing oneself to sense the faint indications of which 'direction' to float your consciousness in, allowing yourself to drift in that direction, allowing yourself to abandon your preconceptions of what you will find.

The directions for this meditation are deliberately rather vague as I do not wish to prejudice you in advance as to your goal. The goal is individual and unique to you and *my* safe harbour is not yours.

Knowing what others have found out while working with this procedure tends to make it more difficult to find your own answers, the only answers with meaning.

Start with twenty-minute periods once a day for two weeks. At that time, if this seems right for you, increase it to a half hour. At the end of another three weeks, you will know if you should continue. I advise not starting with this meditation until after at least a couple of months' serious work with meditations such a breath counting or contemplation.

THE UNSTRUCTURED MEDITATIONS

The meditations presented so far in this chapter are all structured meditations. They are highly precise ways of disciplining the mind with definite patterns of exactly what you do and when you do it. Most of a meditation programme should be composed of this type of discipline. There is another form of meditation, however, of very real importance. This is the unstructured meditation, where you choose an image, a concept, a relationship or a problem and think and feel about it. You stay with the subject chosen, exploring its meaning, its nature and structure and your feelings about it. Again, this is not free association; you stay within the limits of the subject, of the meaning of the subject for you and of how you feel about it. This also is an active process. You are not dazedly day-dreaming about it, but actively exploring and working at it. There will and should be periods in which you observe the flow of your own associations (so long as they stay inside the prescribed limits), but these must not take a majority of the time devoted to the work. Most of your time the active will to know, to comprehend the subject and your relation to it, must be the master of the chariot, must direct the process actively and firmly.

The variety of subjects one can mediate on in this way is very large. You choose a subject that has meaning for you in your quest to grow and develop and to integrate all the parts of you. Frequently you select an area that you feel lags behind the rest of what you are and choose a subject for meditation that will expand and help this area to develop further toward its potential. A subject is chosen to help you toward your goals. Thus many Christian monastics, with their deep vocation of the search for the ability to love God, frequently chose subjects relating to love, to the beauty and glory of God, to the love of Christ, to their own fear of loving and being loved, etc.

The unstructured meditations presented here are examples that are useful for many Westerners. If they make sense and feel right to you, try them and work with them. Otherwise choose your own.

Once you choose an unstructured meditation, do not change it lightly. Work with it for ten to fifteen minutes a day for a week. Then unless you find it actively unsympathetic, increase this time to twenty minutes or a half hour for another week or preferably two. At the end of that time – certainly not before – you will know where you stand with it and whether and how to proceed further.

Sometimes during an unstructured meditation you will come on an understanding that is clearly the answer to be found in this particular session. You will know it when you do. When this happens, stay with the understanding for a few moments. Do not strive to probe more deeply; rather, absorb it, let yourself comprehend it. Then end the session and simply, as you do at the end of every session of meditation, rest quietly for a few moments without a programme.

During the course of working with one of these meditations you may come to the answer you are seeking at this stage of your development. Again, you will be aware of this if it occurs. When this happens follow the procedure given in the previous paragraph and the next day do another session on the same meditation. At the end of this, you should be aware of how to continue with this meditation or if this is the right place to let it go for a time.

The first of the examples to be given here centres on the question 'How would I be if I were the person I would like to be?' It can also be phrased, 'How could I be if I fulfilled my potential completely?' We know we will never reach the places we aim for, to fully be what we dream of for ourselves, to fulfill our potential wholly. However, we can – and we hope *will* – work all our lives toward achieving this end, toward getting closer and closer to the unattainable. What kind of a person would I be if I were the person I deeply wish to be? If all the potentials in me were fulfilled, how would I be, relate, create, act, feel? How do I feel about being this person? What about it attracts me, frightens me? What leads me toward this end and what draws me back?

For many people this is a useful unstructured meditation and helps us clarify our path, inner vocation, hopes, dreams and fears.

A second meditation of this type that is often useful centres on the question 'How do I love?' or 'How would I like to be able to love?' Here we deal with a crucial aspect of life and being for many people of our time. It is in the ability to love that more of us feel weak and crippled than probably in any other area. How *do* I love? Do I wish I could love more? What makes me wish this? What holds me back? What do I fear in loving? How valid are these fears? What does all this mean for the other aspects of my life?

There is a statement made by Teilhard de Chardin in his *The Divine Milieu* that could be useful to some people as an unstructured meditation: 'All the consciousnesses of my life are one consciousness.'

One unstructured meditation is a quotation from Meister Eckhart and is useful for a wider variety of people and situations than one might expect. I have heard it recommended by Pir Vilayat Khan among others. It goes, 'The eye by means of which God sees me is the same eye by means of which I see God.'

Another example of an unstructured meditation you may find relevant and useful is, 'If I were really my best friend, how would I treat myself? How would I feel about being treated in this way?' Again, this is the constant revolving around the two centres: What are the facts? How do I feel about them?

None of these meditations are 'easy' or 'gentle' ones. They hold the possibility of shaking you up more than you expect. They must be done with persistence and also courage, courage to face the unexpected in you and to look at it and attempt to let yourself comprehend it. Freud once wrote, 'The essence of analysis is surprise.' This is not only true of analysis, but, in some ways, of all growth. Heraclitus said, 'If we do not expect the unexpected, we will never find it.' I would add only 'expect *and try and welcome*' to this statement.

ALLURING TRAPS IN MEDITATION AND MYSTICISM

The path of meditation and mystical training is a way of personal development and, if intelligently and seriously followed, will provide growth and bring you further along toward the twin goals outlined in Chapter 3. But it is far from foolproof. It has probably as many traps as psychotherapy and probably as many opportunites for error and self-defeating behaviour as other paths of growth do.

Evelyn Underhill, one of the wisest modern mystics and probably the most learned in mystical literature, has written on this point. In part she says, 'A mystic is not necessarily a perfect human being; and the imperfections and crudities of his character and outlook may influence and mingle with his mysticism. He may at times be feverishly emotional or lacking in genial appreciation of his fellows; he may be too narrowly intense, combative, intolerant.'[1]

Many mystics of both East and West have fallen into a variety of the traps implicit in the path. These include those in strong training traditions and those working alone. As examples of this, I might mention Nikos Kazantzakis's account of the centres on Mount Athos, Arthur Koestler's descriptions of some of the Indian mystics of today. Thomas Merton's discussions of the needs of modern Christian monasticism, and newspaper accounts of what happened at the First International Yoga Conference in India in 1970.[2]

I would like to describe here some of the major traps that some people in the modern human potential movement – the group in this country that has been most seriously interested in meditation and mysticism – have fallen into. These are probably the most common pitfalls on the path at the present time. We certainly did not invent these traps, however. As we look back at the history of mysticism, we can see strong evidence that people have been falling into them for a long time. Some climbed back out. Some did not.

'VIBRATIONS', 'ENERGY', AND OTHER CHEAP EXPLANATIONS OF THINGS

One of the factors making it hardest to keep a commonsense viewpoint about this field and experiences in it is the frequent confusion about the difference between scientific language and mythical language. Because of the difficulty in expressing in scientific language many of the concepts and experiences, we use mythic language, poetry and metaphor. This is fine and useful. The difficulty, however, is that we then frequently confuse the two and believe that the metaphor expressed a real fact. It is clear, as Santayana points out in his *Reason in Science*,[3] that if we say that 'punishment, limping on one leg, patiently follows each criminal,' we do not mean that each criminal is literally followed by a sword-carrying angel with a twisted ankle. This, however, is frequently the error we make in this field. As an example, let us take the 'chakras'. These are, according to various Eastern traditions, specific body locations, energy centres, organs in the etheric body, etc., that are *real* and have a real anatomical location and can be treated and 'energized' or what have you in definite ways. Let me describe two approaches to these, one that kept its metaphors as metaphors, one that did not.

Plato, in *The Republic*,[4] states that he wishes to discuss the nature of a man and his best development, and to do this he will use the analogy of a city. There are three main currents of force in the city, says Plato: the generative forces (artisans and peasants); the vital, emotional forces (the soldiers); the intellectual-spiritual forces (the philosopher-kings). He then goes on in detail as to how these currents can each be developed to their fullest potential and integrated in the greatest harmony possible with the others. Because of

Plato's clarity of thinking and writing, we are not about to point to someone's body and say, 'where are the soldiers actually located?' They are metaphors, myths.

In Taoism, however, the situation starts in the same way and really ends up somewhere else. The Taoists start to discuss the nature of a man and say that it has three basic currents. The generative currents, the vital-emotional currents, and the intellectual-spiritual currents. So far there is a similarity, but now, as is typical in Eastern traditions, the difference between scientific language (which tells you something and deals with facts) and mythic language (which reveals something about how you feel and respond) begins to break down.[5] Taoism locates the source of the generative forces midway between genitals and navel, the vital-emotional forces in the heart area, and the intellectual-spiritual forces in the head. Presently these become real *things* located in these areas (or at least real things in the 'etheric body,' whatever *that* is), and we get the idea we can manipulate these things. Metaphors have become 'facts', chakras now 'exist' and are real; concretistic thinking and a magical orientation have triumphed over our hope of making serious progress.

It must not be forgotten that the mystical schools were begun and developed by some of the greatest of our race, men of courage, wisdom and insight. However, it must also not be forgotten that these men grew up in primitive societies where the thinking was shot through with magical ideas, and was generally pretty concretistic. (Essentially, 'concretistic' means not being able to tell the difference between a metaphor and a fact, between mythic and scientific concepts.) No one really transcends the limitation of his society, although the great minds see somewhat beyond it and help the society progress to new levels. These great men, and certainly their disciples, however, could not go much beyond the concretistic thinking and magical orientations of their cultures. They simply did not have the long background of scientific thought that we have. They also lacked the work of the men who have patiently explored for us the structure of language and thought to give us the tools in this area that we now have. The combination of the genius of the men who founded and developed the meditational methods and the scientific techniques we have since developed can enable us to go further than we would with only one of these.

To do this, however, we must avoid the great seductiveness of confusing mythic language and scientific language. The myth is crucial for evaluation and communication. The fact is also crucial, but the two are not to be confused except with the certainty of seriously hampering any future progress.

If, in a meditation, I feel a tingling in my hands and legs (a fairly typical example of Makyo, a type of hallucination that frequently appears in certain types of meditation), it is legitimate to say that I feel as if there were a lot of energy in my extremities. This is a good and useful metaphor. However, to then go on and say that a meditation of this sort increases the energy in my hands and feet is switching levels, and we now have made a metaphor (revealing our experience) into a fact (which says something is real). The next thing we know we are setting up elaborate electronic equipment to record and measure this 'energy' we have invented and have convinced ourselves of its existence. When the electronic equipment fails to record the energy we either buy *more* delicate equipment or eventually invent something like an 'etheric body' to account for the place the energy 'really is' – and so on until we are completely involved in confusion.

I wish the above were an exaggeration of what happens when we begin to fall into this trap. Unfortunately, it is not. 'Energy' is probably the most widely misused term by meditational schools and students today. More experiences are 'explained' by it and more idiotic conclusions drawn from these explanations than any other term I know. Henry Margenau, one of the leading theoretical physicists of our time, has written in this area, 'Similarly the term energy which has a perfectly definite scientific meaning is constantly used in phrases such as 'mental energy' which signifies nothing unless ignorance of the laws of physics on the part of the speaker.'[6]

Recently a highly-trained scientist, who had also been fairly well

trained in meditational techniques, was leading a movement meditation. In this she instructed the group to 'let your fatigue drain
through the soles of your feet into the earth. Now draw up energy
from the centre of the earth.' I suggested that she would be making
more sense if she let the group know that these were metaphors and
they should 'try to feel as if your fatigue is draining . . . etc.' She
insisted that they were not metaphors but facts, and that she could
not, *in conscience*, present the exercise any other way. And this, mark
you, was a mature and extremely able individual with wide reading
and training behind her. Sometimes this is a pretty discouraging
field! That confusions of this sort can occur thirty years after the
work of Cassirer staggers the mind.

There is certainly a seductiveness in this kind of thinking. It is
easy, pleasant and exciting. It leads to all sorts of interesting beliefs
and brightens up the universe no end. It also saves us the labour of
really trying to be clear in our thinking and of doing the hard mental
work that is called for if we wish to understand our experiences and
the world we live in. In short, it is a pretty cheap cop-out. It is also a
very common one.

There are many other terms used in the same way as the worst
present-day offender, 'energy'. The word 'vibration' is used
frequently in very confused ways. Frequently these are ways that
sound beautiful and useful until you really begin to try to think
about what the person using them really is describing. Then you
wonder if he is crazy or if you are so uptight and conventionally
bound in your thought processes that you cannot see all the lovely
realities that everyone else, nodding their heads in agreement and
admiration, obviously can. Usually you are tempted to follow the
example of the courtiers when the Emperor's new clothes were
being displayed and agree that you can see the chakras, Kundalini
forces, etheric bodies, energy streams and God knows what else. You
are then involved in beautiful poetry and have completely confused
it with reality. Unfortunately this does not lead to the advancement
of knowledge or to your own growth and development.

If a man tells me that his heart resonates to a different rate of vibration than does his liver, I feel that he is telling me something valid. He *is*, he is telling me something valid about his own experience of his body. However, because it does reflect experience, what he says sounds so 'right' and 'reasonable' that I am strongly tempted to interpret it as factual, to believe that the vibrations and resonators he is talking about actually exist and operate the way he says they do. I am very likely to accept all this as 'real'. It is only later when I sit back and try and figure out what these words mean, what their referents are – in short, what the hell we were talking about – that I realize I have not the faintest idea. This is valid mythic and poetic language; it is *not* valid scientific language. The confusion between these two kinds of language has been one of the great disaster areas of meditation and mysticism.

MONDAY IS BLUE, IS SUBATOMIC, IS REGRESSIVE, AND OTHER SILLY MAPS OF REALITY

One of the most typical nonsense trips in the mystical field is another curious mixing up of levels of reality. Because there is a valid way of conceptualizing reality in which everything is related to, and a part of, anything else, mystical schools frequently decide that this also applies to the 'everyday' or 'normal' view of reality. They therefore make charts showing this relationship which they have decided exists. Thus one may, as in the example heading this section, decide 'Monday' is related to the colour 'blue' and to tendencies that are 'regressive', and so forth. (This example is found in a chart of the Africa school of mystical training.) Primitive thinking of this sort leads inevitably to the type of belief that holds that the amethyst increases concentration and the emerald induces chastity. Of course, the particular characteristics you relate to each day or colour depend on your local cultural history and your personality situation. It does not much matter, however, one combination is as good as another.

Of course there is a valid principle here. All events and unities *are* connected; there is nothing that is not related to everything else. The universe is not (from any coherent metaphysical system) made up of isolated, uncaused events. If these charts were designed as teaching devices to help us understand this and to understand the consequent implications – that how we treat one another affects all of us, that the maltreatment of one child darkens the whole world, and that what hurts one sentient being hurts all of us – if this were the purpose and design of the charts and diagrams, then no one could validly criticize them. But they are *not* designed for this purpose. If they were, it would be plain that it is as realistic to say Monday is related to 'red' or 'polka-dotted' as to 'blue'. In my own experience, whether Monday is 'regressive' or not is more dependent on my weekend activities than it is on any deeply profound cosmic order.

THE GAME OF WITHDRAWAL FROM THE WORLD (OR, 'I AM SUCH A HIGH PERSON THAT I CAN SEE THAT YOUR PAIN IS ILLUSION')

A frequent trap in mystical schools has been the idea of withdrawal from relationships with others and from active participation in the world in order to save or develop your own soul. This never took much root in the West. Beyond a brief excursion with the early Desert Fathers, on which the Church rather quickly put its foot, Western mysticism has never dabbled much in this direction. It has been, rather, as the anonymous author of *The Cloud of Unknowing* (a great medieval manuscript on mysticism) demanded it be, 'listy' (the opposite of 'listless'), active, eager, involved. Literally, as Thomas Merton puts it, the Western monk retires to the cloister to become *more* involved in the world, not to retreat from it.

Saint John of the Cross wrote in his 'Ascent of Mt Carmel,' 'How much more in God's sight is one work or act of the will performed in charity than are all the visions and communications they may receive from heaven.' Similarly, in the Hebrew mystical tradition, this trip was rejected. Typical of the Hasidic view, Rabbi Nahman of Bratislava wrote, 'If the holy man seeks only God and does not teach the multitude, he shall descend from whatever rung of the ladder of perfection he has ascended to.'

There is the well-known medieval story of the monk who prayed for many years for a vision of the Virgin. One day, while he was praying in his cell, the vision appeared. At that moment the monastery bell rang, signalling the hour when the poor were fed at the monastery gate. It was his duty to serve them the food. In a terrible quandary the monk left his cell and went to his work. When, several hours later, he returned, the vision was still there and said to him, 'If you had stayed, I must have fled.' Meister Eckhart summed up the Catholic viewpoint by writing, 'If you were in an ecstasy as deep as that of St Paul and there was a sick man who needed a cup of soup, it were better for you that you returned from the ecstasy and brought the cup of soup for love's sake.'

However, in the East, this self-defeating path has often been followed. The first schools of Buddhism were Hinyana Buddhism. Hinyana means 'little ferryboat'; only nuns and priests, those who devoted their entire lives to their own growth and withdrew from the world for it, could ride. Presently it became clear that the results of following this path left a great deal to be desired. Frequently the devotees of Hinyana Buddhism turned out to be calm, centred, intelligent philosophers who could watch starvation and avoid involvement with those starving, since they believed involvement would bind them more closely to the 'wheel of things' and so prevent their inner development.

After a long period of experimentation with this path, Buddhism generally rejected it and turned from Hinyana to Mahayana Buddhism. Mahayana means 'big ferryboat', and the big boat does not leave until every sentient being is aboard. In the clear statement of this turn, Buddhism signalled the end of the withdrawal from this egocentric trip of mysticism. Of the twelve original schools of Hinyana Buddhism, only two remain and these are fairly small.

Frequently today, the meditational approach is interpreted to mean that one should give up involvement in the world and active relationship and participation in it in order to advance one's own development. This is similar to a viewpoint which held sway in psychoanalysis for many years, that all serious decisions should be put off until the analysis was finished. The error in this only gradually became apparent. The essence of a healthy emotional and mental life is action and decision-making, taking conscious control of your own destiny. This is not accomplished by refusing action. Similarly, one's own inner development, which exists in relation to others and the cosmos as well as to the self, is not furthered by a retreat from this relationship. To try to advance part of your development at the expense of other parts only fragments you more and makes you less rather than more complete. Since your relationships with others are a part of your being human, giving them up makes you less whole. Krishnamurti, in discussing the idea of withdrawal from the world in order to find oneself, put his viewpoint succinctly, 'How do you discover what you are? Only in relationship, in communication with another.'[7]

Certainly it is sometimes necessary to step away from others – in the Buddhist phrase, 'go to the mountains' – and retreat for a short time in order to concentrate on one or another aspect of your total growth. The full-time attention to oneself is often helpful and sometimes necessary. It should be plain, however, that the retreat is in order to return fuller and more complete and is of comparatively short duration. In Krishna's words in the Bhagavad-Gita, 'Freedom from activity is never achieved by abstaining from action.'

GREAT WHITE LIGHTS AND HOW TO AVOID THEM

There is the story, repeated in every major mystical training school, of the student who sees great deep visions during his meditations and is told by his teacher to ignore them. A Zen version concerns the student of the Zen master Dogen. The student reported that, deep in his meditation, he had suddenly seen a great white light with the Buddha behind it. 'That's nice,' replied Dogen. 'If you concentrate on your breathing it will go away.'

In the Hesychast tradition we have the warning of the patriarch Callistus, 'The devil approaches contemplatives by producing certain fantasies, at times colouring the air to resemble lights, at others producing flamelike forms in order to tempt the worker in Christ.'

And Ignatius Loyola put it, 'Visions must never be desired or demanded . . . one must, to the limits of one's power, shun them and look upon them with suspicion.'

A Hasidic version concerns Rabbi Nahman of Bratislava when he was a student of Rabbi Elimelekh. Rabbi Nahman told his teacher that in the mornings he got so deeply into his devotions that he could see the angel that rolled away the darkness before the light and in the evening the angel that rolled away the light before the darkness. Rabbi Elimelekh replied, 'Yes, when you are young you see such things. As you continue to work you stop seeing them.'

In the Christian tradition is the account of the students of Saint Philip Neri, who told him of the delicious vision of the Virgin Mary that came to them during their devotions. Saint Philip, who tended to be a rather dramatic individual, advised them that the next time she appeared, they were to spit in her face! According to the account they did so and she never reappeared.

Why should a tale like this be told in every serious mystical school? It is a cautionary tale, warning against one of the most common traps of the meditational path: the trap of interest in exciting phenomena. Once the meditator falls into this, whether it be the search for 'Great, White Lights,' or for ESP phenomena, or for high ecstatic states, he is almost certain to lose sight of his real goal, his inner growth and becoming. There is the story, in the Pali Canon (a manuscript of ancient Buddhism) of a disciple who showed the Buddha a tremendous feat of levitation he had perfected over many year's study. The Buddha replied dryly that it would not further serious matters and returned to his discussion of inner development.

Meditation does often produce high feelings and unusual perceptions. This is fine if they are treated according to the Zen method, 'If you concentrate on your breathing, it will go away.' Essentially, there are two causes for the special perceptions, such as great white lights. (In the East they are most typically great white lights. In the Christian mystical tradition the lights are often coloured and frequently accompanied by music. How one of these illusions manifests itself is partly determined by your cultural background.)

The first of these two causes is the Makyo reason described on page 49. These are a part of your resistance to the hard discipline of meditation. It is a way the sailors, in Plato's analogy of the mutiny, attempt to prevent the Captain from resuming command. As a manoeuvre to maintain the mutiny, it is often successful. A large number of individuals getting into meditation become so entranced and interested in these phenomena that all interest in serious work is lost.

The second cause of these phenomena is a sudden awareness that we are looking at things and responding to them differently than we did in the past. This can come as quite a shock and we can react to it both psychologically and physically – with a sudden experience of light, with unusual perspiration, or with a wonderful, 'high' feeling. These are nice when they happen and the advice of every serious meditational school is the same: enjoy them, do not take them very seriously, get back to work!

Unfortunately, many in the group interested in meditation have fallen into one version of this trap and become remarkably anti-intellectual. Ideas, knowledge, intelligence are downgraded and disregarded in favour of experiences and of emotional and bodily expression. They say, in effect, 'We will only become whole by discarding part of ourselves and our heritage. Down with the cortex.' Their rebellion against being overcerebralized has led them to the opposite extreme, leading to a fragmentation equal to the one they were escaping. So far has this gone (this is hard to believe, but unfortunately true) that some start the practice of psychotherapy without ever studying the tremendously rich background of psychology and psychiatry that the West has to offer. From my own viewpoint, a therapist who has not had wide experiences in life and is not in contact with his own emotions is essentially sterile, and one who has not read widely in Freud, Jung, Adler and a couple of dozen others is the equivalent of an aeroplane designer who has not studied calculus.

Behind the frequency with which meditators fall into this trap today lies an attitude on the part of many in the human potential movement that can seriously interfere with real growth; namely, that it is good and worthwhile for its own sake to get 'high'; that being in an ecstatic or semi-ecstatic state is of value in itself.

The absolute validity of this attitude cannot be defended or attacked. It is part of a philosophy of life and as such can only be dealt with in that total context. What *can* be said is that from the viewpoint of inner growth, the striving to reach one's fullest potential as a human being, such an attitude is contradictory. Every serious school of mediation, every serious school of psychotherapy, has pointed out that such seeking after sensation for its own sake slows down or prevents inner development rather than enhances it. The statement of Saint John of the Cross, that as soon as signs of an approaching ecstasy are manifested, one should turn one's attention to other things, is similar to statements made in every other school.

Certainly a high state may occasionally be of real value in showing us what we are working toward, in helping to strengthen our motivation to carry us over the long, hard, dry periods. Walter Huston Clark put it, 'Drugs can open a door, but do not give us room to live in.' A really good LSD trip may bring us high on the mountain, so we can see the outskirts of the promised land we strive for. Then, however, we are faced with a choice. Do we stay on the mountain with the aid of more LSD, or do we descend to the base and face the long discipline of crossing the desert to really get there? Each person must make the choice for himself.

My Guru Is Higher Than Your Guru

I have referred earlier to the fads and fashions in mysticism and meditation. It is certainly true that in as serious a matter as the one we are
discussing it is important to learn from many people, not just from
one. If you went to a medical school, you would expect to have more
than one professor. The difficulty in this field is that generally those
who go from school to school, guru to guru, technique to technique
are expressing their own resistance to the real, long-term discipline
involved in inner growth. As they bounce from one 'master' to
another they are demonstrating the truth of a statement of Sri
Chinmoy (a teacher of meditation) when he wrote, 'Some people will
do anything for their own advancement except work for it.'

With all this constant moving from one 'answer' to another, this
constant searching for the ideal and quick way to 'enlightenment',
this striving to find a 'perfect master' (isn't *that* concept a wild one?
How Alfred Korzybski, the founder of the General Semantics, would
have loved it), a good deal of competition and rivalry enters the picture.
There is more and more comparing of gurus and teachers, and having
the 'right' or the 'in' teacher of meditation techniques becomes a
matter of status rather than a quiet inner searching for the best in
oneself. 'You're still doing the Zen trip? That was last year. I'm now
doing the American Indian shaman trip. *That's* where it's at now.'

Further, this tends to affect the gurus. Anybody who sets up shop
as a guru is likely to have so much of his status needs involved in his
guruship that he is pretty vulnerable to getting into competition
with others similarly involved. Oscar Ichazo, an experienced teacher
of meditation with a wide knowledge of the field, pointed out to me
that once a person thinks of himself as a guru and allows this
thinking to influence (as it must) his human relationships, the
approach he is using inevitably turns sour. Not only is the little spark
of vanity that always remains in each of us overfed, but no one tells
him when he is behaving badly or stupidly. Without necessary negative feedback from others, his judgment becomes badly impaired.[8]

There are now so many completely unqualified people declaring themselves qualified to guide you to the higher reaches of the enlightenment stratosphere that the whole field has become pretty messy. The amount of kooiness rampant in it seems to be increasing in geometric progression. Jack Gariss, in a well-done little pamphlet, *A Beginner's Guide to Meditation*, has given a pretty good picture of one aspect of this field as . . .

> . . . *a confusing, if exotic, metaphysical mart where priest, guru, avatar and master display their meditative wares and whisper down their competitors. The only technique, some say, is to fix your attention upon a single object: candle, picture, cross, mandala, or third eye. Others will smile condescendingly at such naïveté. The secret as handed from the master, they inform you in hushed tones, is to concentrate upon the mental image of the beloved master. Only they disagree gently whether that master be Jesus, Buddha, Krishna or a Shakti engaged in carnal embrace with Shiva.*
>
> *Such divergent advice like contrasting perfumes of incense drift about the religious stalls. Repeat aloud continuously a sacred sound, mantra or prayer. No, not aloud! Repeat silently the sacred sound, mantra or prayer until only the vibration carries through the successive layers of consciousness to God consciousness or Bliss consciousness. Meditate near the ocean. Meditate near a waterfall. Meditate in silence. Count your beads. Count your breath. Never count your breath.* [9]

One learns from many people. There is no one right path for everyone and no ideal way to grow and become. If you remember that you are looking for the most of yourself you can find and that this is a task for adults, you will be able to smile sadly as the spiritual athletes (a far cry from the medieval monastics, who termed themselves the 'athletes of God') chase the baubles of status, the myth of 'enlightenment', and the hope of something for nothing, from one perfect master to another.

Is a Teacher Necessary for Meditation? Choosing Your Own Meditational Path

One of the first questions that usually arises in discussions of meditation is the necessity for a teacher. There are many specialists in meditation who believe that serious work without a teacher is impossible. When you ask these specialists 'Who taught the first teacher?' the answers generally fall into four classes. One group says that the first teacher was enlightened by God. The second group says you cannot understand the answer until you have studied (usually with this specialist himself) for a number of years. The third group gets angry. None of these answers is particularly constructive. The fourth group says that the techniques of meditation were worked out empirically over long periods of time and that it takes too long for any one individual to be able to repeat their work. This answer to the question is, I believe, an intelligent and serious one even if I do not completely agree with it.

My own belief is that a teacher can be very helpful with all forms of meditation but is probably most essential if one is following the route of the body, the middle way, or the route of action. For the route of the intellect or of the emotions, a good teacher can certainly help speed up your progress, but is not really necessary. There is enough clear written material on these routes that can be followed.

Overall, no teacher is probably better than one who is not good, who is not skilled at the theory and technique of meditation, who is concerned with *his* goals rather than *yours*, who does not evaluate and help each student as an individual. Unless you can communicate clearly with a teacher and receive answers relevant to your questions and goals, it is better to look elsewhere. A good teacher accepts and celebrates where you are now, joins you in and clarifies your dreams for yourself, and helps you as a guide and adviser on the road to their attainment. Saint Thérèse of Lisieux, writing of this, put it from the viewpoint of a Catholic spiritual director: 'I know it seems easy to help souls, to make them love God above all and to mould them according to His will. But actually, without His help, it is easier to make the sun shine at night. One must banish one's own tastes and personal ideas and guide souls along the special way Jesus indicates for them rather than along one's own particular way.'[1]

Further, what kind of person is the teacher? One (I hope) would not got to a psychotherapist who had severe neurotic problems. Similarly one should evaluate a meditation teacher. If the techniques for inner growth, be they psychotherapy or meditation or what have you, make any sense and work, they should have worked with someone who knows them enough to guide you. Few of us would go to a gymnasium instructor with a soft, flabby body. Look at the teacher and see what his approach and work have done for *him*. Arthur Deikman, a psychiatrist who knows a great deal about meditation, has designed what he humorously calls The Deikman Test of Spiritual Advancement. It has one deadly question: 'How does he get along with his wife?' The question, of course, is about more than just a relationship with a spouse. It really asks 'What are his human relationships?' 'How does he relate to other people?' If these relationships are not of the kind you admire, then it really does not matter how steadily he looks at you from behind his steely grey eyes, how silently he sits in a perfect lotus position, or how impressive he looks in robe and beard. Cross him off your list and look elsewhere.

Another aspect of your evaluation should involve the question of the teacher's commitment to the 'guru trip'. A few moments of discussion will quickly make it plain if this is what he is on. If he implies that you should simply follow directions for the next several (or more) years without asking why, but trust him, and then you will arrive at the promised land also and be enlightened, he is on a guru trip. For all I know, this approach may have sometimes been quite meaningful in second-century India or tenth-century Japan, but it is certainly not meaningful for Westerners today. We are not (unless we are pretty confused) about to put our brains in the deep freeze for years and years in order to grow. Among other things, it fragments us even more to discard our heads when we are striving to achieve wholeness and less fragmentation. In the Kalama Sutra, a statement attributed to the Buddha clearly warns us to evaluate serious matters ourselves and not to just 'trust' a guru:

> *Do not believe on the strength of traditions even if they have been held in honour for many generations and in many places; do not believe anything because many people speak of it; do not believe on the strength of sagas of old times; do not believe that which you have imagined, thinking a god has inspired you. Believe nothing which depends only on the authority of your masters or of priests. After investigation, believe that which you yourself have tested and found reasonable, and which is for your good and that of others.*[2]

If a guru tells you that he is imparting 'secret' knowledge reserved for special people (like you) and that you must swear never to reveal it to the uninitiated, I advise seeking the nearest exit immediately. Can you imagine a Socrates, a Jesus, a Buddha, telling his disciples that his wisdom was to be kept secret? It is, of course, very flattering and exciting to be told that you are part of the small band of the select who are fit to be given the deep 'truths', but it is hardly realistic and certainly is not helpful to your own growth! In addition, anyone who promises you meditation training, inner growth and development, and then organizes the process as a big business – as do various organizations now in existence – is operating on a basis opposite to every known reasonable principle in the field.

Pir Vilayat Khan, a wise and experienced Sufi leader, was speaking recently on the matter of relationships with a guru.[3] He pointed out that one should be very careful in selecting a teacher, and that if a guru told you what to do, this would ' weaken your ability to come to your own decisions and that is what the work is all about.' Pir Vilayat quoted Rumi that 'the real guru is one who has killed the idol you have made of him.' This, of course, implies that the teacher who finds his own status and worth in a relationship in which the student looks up to and uncritically obeys him is not a teacher to work with. Further, he went on, one should learn from many people, not just one, no matter how wise he is. And, in this area, 'never accept anything less than the best.'

What we are really talking about here is the essence of all good human relationships. We can – and must if we would change and grow – learn from other people, but we do not select one and let him programme us as if we were a computer. We listen to others and learn from their knowledge and experience, but the crucial test of advice and suggestions is 'Does this make sense and feel right to *me*?' Only if the answer to this question is 'yes' do we follow the suggestion, only if it is the idea we sense we were looking for to move further on our quest but did not know where to find. Similarly, we stay with a teacher, *as* a teacher, only so long as we grow through the relationship, then move on.

A teacher, be he called 'adviser', 'experienced friend', 'guide', 'guru' or 'spiritual director', is a tremendous help if he fulfills the qualifications I have described and if your relationship is a good human relationship. He will save you time, help to avoid problems or solve them more quickly, and encourage you to stay with it when you become dispirited, as you will if you pursue the way of meditation seriously.

If you do decide, for whatever reasons, to work alone, there are certain guidelines that may be useful. Here are some of them.

In planning a meditational programme for yourself, a critical element is being realistic. How much time *will* you spend on this discipline is the first question, not how much time you would *like* to spend on it. An important aspect of meditation is follow-through, keeping your promises to yourself. Short of an emergency, it is a part of the programme that you finish each meditation you start in the form you started it and that you finish each plan for a programme of meditation in the form you planned it. For this reason it is necessary to be realistic about the amount of time you will spend on a programme. Take into account what kind of a person you are now (rather than the kind of person you wish you were) and how busy and complex your life is, and plan accordingly. The suggested programmes for the route of the intellect and the route of the emotions that are given later in this chapter can serve as guidelines on planning your time.

You will be disappointed if you expect immediate, dramatic results. Growth and serious change do not come this way no matter what techniques or approaches you use. In this most serious area – inner development – we are interested in evolution, which is stable, rather than revolution, which is not. You will see changes in yourself if you stick to an intelligently planned programme, but they will be gradual.

Not only will the changes be gradual, but you must expect difficult times. As in any serious work, there will be periods during which you feel discouraged, periods in which you seem not only to be making no progress, but actually losing ground. Thomas Merton warns of these when he writes of one of these periods that must often be passed through:

> . . . the case of those who, after having made a satisfactory beginning, experience the inevitable let-down which comes when the life of meditation gets to be serious. What at first seemed easy and rewarding suddenly comes to be utterly impossible. The mind will not work. One cannot concentrate on anything. The imagination and the emotions wander away. Sometimes they run wild . . . unconscious fantasies may take over. They may be unpleasant and even frightening. More often, one's inner life becomes a desert which lacks all interest whatever.[4]

An important point is not to discuss the effects a meditational programme is having on you too much. Don't talk it to death. This is essentially a private matter between you and you. A creative task demands a certain amount of privacy, and meditation is a creative taking hold of and shaping your own life and destiny.

If you choose to follow the path of the intellect, the first part consists of reaching an intellectual understanding of the two ways of perceiving and relating to reality. I suggest that careful reading of several books listed in endnote [5] would be helpful. At the same time, start with Breath Counting. After two to three weeks, add Contemplation. Stay with these two for another three weeks and then add the Lotus meditation. After two or three months of this combination – if done regularly and according to the instructions – you will probably be ready to add the 'Who Am I?' meditation. After a period of a few months of working with these, you should be able to choose a future programme for yourself.

If you decide you would be best working on the route of the emotions, I would suggest the following combination of meditations. Start with Breath Counting for the basic discipline needed. After a few weeks of this, add the Bubble meditation. Then after another three to four weeks, complete the series by adding the 'How Do I Love?' and/or 'What is the best in me?' unstructured meditations. After another four weeks, add the 'Safe Harbour' meditation or, if time is a crucial factor, substitute it for the unstructured meditations or for the Bubble meditation. After a few months of this programme, followed consistently, you should be ready to either continue the programme as it is or else to redesign it to your own needs.

If you find that Breath Counting does not generally appear to make you feel better and more 'together' (more coherent and organized) after giving it a try for two or three weeks, change to the Mantra meditation for this part of the programme.

The route of the body is difficult to follow without a good teacher, although it can be done. If you feel this is your best route, work with the Sensory Awareness meditation and/or that of the Dervish dance. If these go well and make sense for you after the necessary two or three weeks of trying them out, then continue them and after another month add variations on these themes you design yourself.

There are also teachers for some of these techniques available in many cities today. Sensory Awareness is a rapidly growing discipline. In my own experience, teachers trained and approved by Corolla Speads or by Charlotte Selver bring a special quality to their work. Teachers of Tai Chi are also increasing in number at this time.

It is doubtful if the way of action can be taught without a highly skilled teacher. For this reason no exercises of this sort are included in this book. In this country there are available a few Zen masters teaching karate and aikido in this way. In some of the monasteries and monastic retreats there are Spiritual Directors who teach this path through the activity of prayer. For monastics, it may be taught through both prayer and singing as in some of the Benedictine monasteries. Although the path of action is a major one, there are few of the necessary teachers available in the west at this time. If the *Little Way* of Saint Thérèse of Lisieux feels right for you at this time in your development, then by all means follow it. If you have the persistence and courage to stay with it past the long hard, discouraging first part (in the words of Baba Hari Dass, 'The Yoga of house holder is a very hard Yoga'), it is a path of very great value.

No matter what route you choose to follow, it is important that you stay with whatever plan you make. Always plan *at least* three weeks in advance and follow it through. This is a crucial part of the discipline. Meditation is a hard but rewarding road. The game is worth the candle. I hope you will join me on it.

As I have tried to make clear, partly by the use of quotations from many times and places, you are not alone in this search for the fullest and best in yourself. You may work alone, but you work as a member of a great company of other human beings who have followed this path.

Meditation is not something that was invented in – and happened in – history. It is a ageless human experience that has been discovered and explored and used in every period and every culture that we know about. It has always been used by only a few in each place and time, but for those few who have worked seriously at it there has been real gain. It has brought them increased strength and serenity, increased ability to function and find peace and joy.

Some have worked in schools of esoteric training, the mystical schools of East and West. Working in a tradition, whether it be Zen, Yoga, Sufi, Hasidism, Christian mysticism, or the lesser-known traditions, such as the one of Don Juan which Carlos Castaneda so beautifully and expertly describes in his books,[6] has advantages and disadvantages. Some advantages are the clearly marked out paths and training sequences for the students to follow. There are also teachers to help and encourage and to warn in advance of the worst traps, or to help you if you fall into them. As a disadvantage, they mostly tend to believe that their particular path and goal are the only valid ones and that the student must adapt to them rather than the other way around. (Don Juan's approach seems a clear exception to this.)

Is it better to work alone or in a school? There is no clear answer to this question. It is certainly better to work by yourself than to work with a teacher or a school that is not right for you, that does not relate to *your* personality, *your* needs, *your* goals. If you find a teacher or a school that does relate to you in these ways, it will however, probably go much better, more easily and more rapidly for you than if you work alone.

There is also another possibility. That is to work with a small group of like-minded people. If you can find some others who feel as you do about the search and can work together once or a couple of times a week, you may very well find very great advantages in this method. Mutually you encourage each other, and help each other over the dry and difficult times. You are much less likely to stop working when you share the process with others. You learn from each other if you share experiences and often a problem that one person cannot seem to solve is solved easily by another in the group. The next month the process of who helps who is likely to be reversed.

It is important in this kind of work with a group to learn from each other, but not to be bound or limited by each other. Work together as well as alone. Use the same meditations when they are right for each of you and different ones when this is indicated by who and where you are. Do not expect or demand that you have the same experiences; if the process is alive and creative there will be some experiences that are shared and many that are not. The most meaningful ones in your own growth may be either shared or unshared. The purpose of the group is to help each individual in his growth, not to set up standards of what kinds of experiences to have and when to have them. Nor is its purpose to set up categories and hierarchies between members. If you find yourselves getting into competitions of experiences, considering that one person is growing better than another in the group, you are in the beginning of a bad trip. It is time then to sit down for a talk with all the members of the group and to re-examine your goals. You may find that you are no longer following them.

Perhaps this is the most important thing – whether you work alone, in a group, with a teacher or in a school – to remain clear as to your purpose, to remain clear that the discipline is to help you find, accept and sing the best in you, a best that is unique, individual and yours alone. A best that you share with all those of the human race who, in one way or another, have made the search, but that is for each person something different and special. It is this goal and search that every great philosophy and religion believe are the highest and best things a human being can do and are the ultimate delight of God.

THE INTEGRATION OF PSYCHOTHERAPY AND MEDITATION:
A Set of Guidelines for Psychotherapists

This chapter is somewhat different from the others in this book. It is addressed primarily to the professional psychotherapist who is interested in combining psychotherapy and meditation in his practice. Therefore those who are not particularly interested in the possibilities of such a synthesis can skip directly to Chapter 12, 'The Social Significance of Meditation.'

In the long history of man's attempts to develop procedures that could be used to further personality growth and integration, two basic approaches have been developed that are relevant to the climate of the twentieth century. These two might be called the psychotherapeutic approach and the meditative approach.

The differences between these two methods in origin, technique and goals have appeared to be so great that it is only very rarely that they have been considered together or that the possibility of integrating them has been studied. Meditation developed primarily in environments with a strong religious orientation, psychotherapy in an environment with a strong rationalistic bias. Meditation is essentially a procedure one follows by oneself with rather little direct communication with anyone else. Psychotherapy typically involves very strong interpersonal interaction. The goals of traditional psychotherapy have been to solve special problems of the individual and, in Freud's words, 'return him to that unhappiness general to mankind'; that is, to bring the patient up to normalcy. The goals of traditional meditation have been to try to help the meditator pass beyond what are generally considered to be normal states to help him to a level of being not generally reached by the population at large.

Another set of differences involves emphasis on structure and content. I have discussed this in Chapter 1, but it may bear repetition here. The psychotherapist primarily works with content, only secondarily with structure. The reverse is true with the teacher of meditation. This can, perhaps, be best shown in the typical ways of handling a specific emotional problem. If I go to a psychotherapist with an acute anxiety attack, he will be oriented largely to exploring its content. He will be concerned with the meaning of the anxiety and the theoretical viewpoint will be that, as the content is reorganized in more dynamically healthful ways, the personality structure will become better integrated and balanced.

If, however, with the same anxiety attack I go for help to a teacher of meditation, his primary concern will be with the structure of my personality. Rather than explore content and meaning on different personality levels, he will give me exercises (meditations) designed to strengthen the personality structure. His viewpoint will be that, as the structure is strengthened and made stronger (both overall and in its weakest areas), the content will reorganize itself in a healthy manner and material that is on psychodynamic levels where it causes strain will automatically move to levels where it can aid positive functioning.

It is because of differences such as these that there has been in the past little interest in integrating the two approaches. It may well be, however, that with the new *Zeitgeist* appearing in the West, the time has come to begin to explore the possibilities of such an integration.

With this viewpoint we begin to see similarities as well as differences and understand that the special strengths of each method might be complementary.

There do not seem to be fundamental contradictions in the two methods that would preclude such an integration. As we look at both, a synthesis does not appear to lead to a cognitive dissonance nor to an emotional 'double-bind' situation. No therapist would do other than welcome the addition of procedures that increased ego strength while he explored unconscious content, or of procedures that increased flexibility in a highly rigid patient while he explored the origins and sources of support of this rigidity. No teacher of meditation would object to the exploration and re-evaluation of structure at the same time he worked with the strengthening and buttressing of that personality structure. The religious bias of most, but not all, meditational procedures is in no way inherent in the method (Zen, for example, is completely areligious) any more than the antireligious viewpoint of Freud is a critical cornerstone of psychotherapy. The goals of psychotherapy have been consistently broadening in the past fifty years to include the growth beyond 'normal' that has always been a part of the meditational orientation, and no basic contradiction any longer exists in this area.

The basic model of man that led to the development of meditational techniques is the same model that led to humanistic psychotherapy. In this model we are closer to Rousseau then to Hobbes. Negative behaviour (hate and aggression toward the self and others, destruction of the environment one lives in or of 'the temple of the body,' anxiety and depression, etc) are not seen as the result of natural, inner drives. Man is basically seen as a social animal syntonic with the earth and the cosmos who, because of his anxieties and his training in valuing the wrong things, loses contact with his natural being. It is doubtful if there is a serious teacher of meditation, today or in the past, who would disagree with Maslow's concept of D and B needs, or with Carl Rogers when he wrote, "One of the most revolutionary concepts to grow out of our clinical experience is the growing recognition that the innermost core of man's nature, the deepest levels of his personality, the base of his 'animal nature' is basically socialized, forward-moving, rational and realistic.'[1]

Nor would any serious humanistic psychotherapist disagree with the early Byzantine mystic who advised, 'Whatever you see your soul to desire according to God, do that thing and you shall keep your heart safe.'[2] The crucial phrase is 'according to God' – the deepest part of the being, not the transitory wishes and impulses, what 'the soul' desires, not just the body or impulses. Here is a strong and clear statement of the real meaning of 'do your own thing'.

The statement that self-actualization is a basic human drive, so strongly stated by Kurt Goldstein and by Maslow, is reflected by Pir Vilayat Khan, 'No force anywhere on earth is as imperialistic as the human soul. It occupies and is occupied in turn, but it always considers its empire too narrow. Suffocating, it desires to conquer the world in order to breathe freely.'[3]

If the psychotherapist is using a Freudian model of man, meditational procedures can also be useful for buttressing the ego structure, centering and for exploring specific areas by the patient working alone. The insights gained can be of real use. Since from a Freudian viewpoint, peak and transcendental experiences are viewed as regressive phenomena, it will be the therapist's task to help the patient use these regressions 'in the service of the ego'.

Pir Vilayat Khan put another aspect of this quite strikingly when he said, 'One of the axioms of spiritual realization is doing consciously what would otherwise be done unconsciously.'[4] Examples could be multiplied. Both aim for inner growth and development. Both are designed to help the individual reach his own, special, fullest potential in being, relating, creating. The fact that there are many differences in technique and the fact that both often fail in their goals (partly due to the fact that both are in pretty early and primitive states of the art) should no longer blind us to the similarities or to the possibilities of a useful synthesis.

The basic goals of the two sets of procedures have been much more similar than is generally realized. Each is a method to help the individual to his own solution to the three questions which, said Kant, it is the endeavour of philosophy to answer: What can I know? What ought I to do? What dare I hope?

A statement of Carl Rogers on the direction taken by a person as he responds to psychotherapy would, I believe, be acceptable to any serious teacher of meditation on the course taken as one follows this path:

The person increasingly discovers that his own organism is trust-worthy, that it is a suitable instrument for discovering the most satisfying behaviour in each immediate situation . . . To the extent that this person is open to all of his experience, he has access to all the available data on the situation, on which to base his behaviour. He has knowledge of his own feelings, which are often complex and contradictory . . . He is better able to permit his total organism, his conscious thought participating, to consider, weigh and balance each stimulus, need, and demand, and its relative weight and inten-sity.[5]

This chapter is a discussion of the possible synthesis of these two methods from the viewpoint of the psychotherapist. The problem posed is thus: What are the specific values that meditational proce-dures can bring to my psychotherapeutic approach and what types of meditation would be most useful?

From my own viewpoint, as both a psychotherapist and a teacher of meditation, it seems to me that to the first part of the question (What are the specific values that meditational procedures can bring to my psychotherapeutic approach?) there are five major answers.

The first answer has already been implied. Many meditations bring about an increase in ego strength and in the coherence of personality organization in much the same way as working in a gymnasium brings about the development of the muscles and increases the integration of the muscular apparatus with the breathing and cardiovascular apparatuses. The hard work and intensive discipline of serious meditations make the analogy of a body development programme in a gymnasium not too far-fetched.

The second answer concerns the use of meditations for special problem areas. Very often a meditation can be used to help explore a specific area, to help the patient 'loosen' the defenses of an area and to do some directed exploring of it on his own in a safe, guided and useful manner.

The third answer to the question concerns the process some

meditational teachers have called 'centring'. This refers to the quality of feeling at home and at ease with oneself and with one's environment. The *route* of centring (meditation on the body and its movements, emotional life, physical, social or cosmic environment) will be chosen according to the needs and personality of the patient; the *result* is usually being more at ease and at home in all these areas. The more centred the patient is, the more easily and with less anxiety he will be able to make progress in psychotherapy.

Fourth, both methods have, as part of their primary growth techniques, a consistent programme of teaching the individual to regard his own being as something of real value and to pay serious attention to the totality of his own being. In this programme one learns to respond to and to nurture the best in oneself and also to accept fully the parts one does not regard in this light. As a part of this, rarely verbalized or discussed, but essential for the growth process, meditation can be of much aid to the psychotherapeutic process.

Finally, if our viewpoint in psychotherapy includes a growing beyond the ability to function in everyday life and being relatively 'pain-free', then there is a fifth answer to the question we are looking at. Historically, transcendence experiences have been a major goal of meditational programmes and if we are interested in helping the patient grow to levels where these are a part of his existence, meditations are almost a necessity. In Abraham Maslow's words, 'When we are fully realized under the term "human", transcendence experiences should, in theory, be common.'

Before proceeding to more discussion of these five points, it might be well to look at meditational procedures in general. On surveying their immense number and variety, we are immediately struck by their frequently baroque and rococo quality. They often seem complex and intricate in design. This is true, but by no means useful. The complex quality has been made up by the accretion of additions made by generations of students on basically simple procedures, and the more complex a meditation is, the less useful it is. (As with any rule of thumb, this one also has exceptions, but they are rare.) A good meditation is simple, straightforward and oriented towards a particular problem. If you cannot figure out a simple rationale behind a meditation it is usually best to forget it. Meister Eckhart, a profound student of mystical and meditational procedures, put it, 'The wiser and more skilful a teacher is, the more simply and with less artifice he achieves his ends.'

It does not seem possible, at this early stage of our knowledge, to give more than general guidelines and principles to the psychotherapist designing meditational programmes for his patients. Not only do we know far too little, not only is the amount of experimental (and even anecdotal) material abysmally small, but it would run counter to the crucial general principle that meditational paths are as individual as psychotherapeutic paths and must always be considered in this light. To design standardized programmes for certain categories of patients would lead to an automatized sterility much like that which frequently characterizes mystical training schools when they 'freeze' their procedures, on the assumption that they now know the 'right' way for everyone to meditate.

There are, however, general principles to follow. These include:

1. The therapist prescribing meditations should have had experience – and serious experience – in meditating himself, just as it is necessary for psychotherapists to have had extensive psychotherapy before they open up a practice.

2. Patients progress in psychotherapy most rapidly and effectively from areas of strength and coherence and least rapidly from areas with less of these characteristics. If a major organismic area can be strengthened and brought more into relation and coherence with the rest of the being, psychotherapeutic progress will be aided.

   The different types and routes of meditation increase the strength and integration of different aspects of the total person. On a simplified level, one would think that for patients with little relation to, or joy in, the physical aspects of their being, one might be oriented toward Hatha Yoga, Sensory Awareness, the

Alexander technique, Dervish dances, and meditations of this type. Where the emotional life is undernourished, there might be an orientation toward Bhakti Yoga, meditations of the inner way, some of the Byzantine or Christian monastic techniques and approaches of this kind. Where the intellectual life is under-valued and unexpressed, one might think in the direction of Jnana Yoga, meditations of the outer way, Gurdjieff or Ouspensky training, and so forth. For patients with an inability to work consistently toward goals and to accept the necessary inner discipline to function successfully, one might think in terms of Contemplation, Breath Counting, Mantra work or Zen training. All serious meditational paths – if they are the correct one for *this* individual and if followed consistently – lead ultimately to the same overall growth, but along the way each has its special values. It is in terms of these special strengths and effects that we design meditational programmes for our patients.

It is true that for individuals working in meditation alone, it is advisable to start meditational practices in the area of their greatest strength rather than in an organismic area of weakness (See Chapter 2). I do not, however, believe that this constitutes a contradiction with the suggestions made above. Working alone without the guidance and encouragement of an experienced meditator is discouraging and replete with possibilities of taking useless bypaths. In working in your own area of strength these problems are minimized (as they are maximized in working in your area of weakness). The therapist, serving as the experienced guide, can help you past the problems involved if you were medi-tating on your own.

3. The exploration of particular problems in psychotherapy can be made more rapidly and the effects more related to the person as a whole, thereby making them more permanent, by the use of special meditation procedures related to these problems. It must again be stated that there is really little value in doing a medita-tion once or a few times and this principle holds in this area also.

For it to operate, a meditation must be done as a daily discipline at least for a couple of weeks. Patients should also be warned not to expect or demand that a meditation be the same or 'better' each time they do it. There is great variation, frequently to extremes, and the demand in advance of what a meditation 'should be' leads only to sterility and ritual. In Emerson's words, 'The roses under my window make no reference to former roses or to better ones. They are for what they are.'

Meditations for special problems can come from a variety of types. The Lotus meditation, for example, used by patients for whom the outer way is especially desirable, with a key word or image relating to the area being used as the centre of the lotus, can be very useful. There should, as per the instructions in Chapter 8, be at least half a dozen sessions with this meditation using positive terms as the centre before it is used as a problem-solving meditation. For patients for whom the inner way is desirable, meditations like the Bubble meditation (or the variants described in Chapter 8) can be useful. They would be used, in this type of situation, when the patient is in the midst of the psychotherapeutic work on this problem and is concerned with and oriented toward it.

In many situations unstructured meditations can be useful. The meditation chosen would be related to the problem being explored in psychotherapy. The examples given in Chapter 8 should provide a demonstration of how these are designed. With many patients, however, it must be stressed that these are not periods of day-dreaming about a subject or guided fantasy (which may be valid and helpful psychotherapeutically), but are tough and disciplined in their own way. There is, when working with them, a constant return and 'folding back' to the two key centres, 'What are the facts of the matter?' 'How do I feel about these facts?'

4. 'Centring' techniques can be useful as part of the therapeutic hour or as part of the therapeutic process generally. As part of the

therapeutic hour it can probably be used most effectively in one of two ways, to have the patient use a 'centring' meditation just before or immediately after the hour. (There is, so far as I know, no theoretical reason not to use both.) The use of a before-the-hour period calms and integrates the patient without having him lose the concerns, feelings and drives that he presently is concerned with and needs to bring out. From the centred and more confident position gained by these techniques, the patient is better able to develop and explore his present self. The meditation brings the more relaxed and confident position without the 'blanketing and blanking' effects of tranquillizer drugs.

The purpose of a meditation of this sort (or of a serious meditation of any sort) is not to make the meditator 'feel good'. That is a nice result when it happens, but the purpose is to make him clearer, more focused on, and able to handle how he *does* feel. Generally, of course, this makes the person feel better than he would if he did not do the meditation. This is all to the good, but it must be kept in mind that the real purpose is to make him feel more himself, more integrated to and in command of whatever his internal situation is, not to make him feel *good*.

For the after-the-hour period these meditations can be useful in helping the patient digest and integrate the material and feelings explored in the session. This is a period when other, outside events do not distract him from the material or 'jolt' him so that there is no time for real integration.

As a part of the general therapeutic process, centering done regularly at other times can help increase the sense of being at home with oneself and the world and certainly act as a general way of aiding the psychotherapeutic process.

For centering exercises I would think particularly in terms of Breath Counting, Mantra work, and the Theraveda meditations described in Chapter 8. For some people Contemplation is also quite useful as a centering meditation, but there is particularly wide variation among individuals on this.

5. In designing meditational programmes for patients, a psychotherapist must be realistic and help the patient to be realistic also. The amount of time a programme will take is planned partly on the basis of how much time this particular individual, *as he is now*, will devote to it. The discipline of a meditational practice partially rests on carrying out your commitments to it. It is not good for the programme if it is planned in such a way that it will take more time than this person will give to it.

Secondly, the awareness of the therapist that there is no magic or easy road to serious growth and development must be transmitted to the patient. Attitudes that one will arrive at a sudden enlightenment that will transform one's life completely are unrealistic, silly, and have a negative effect on progress. The course of one's own evolution and development can be aided and speeded up by meditation as it can be by psychotherapy, but both are long and not easy roads.

This theoretical framework and the guidelines offered can serve as a structure for psychotherapists within which we can develop our knowledge of ways to integrate psychotherapeutic and meditational procedures in our attempts to learn more about gardening each other and ourselves. I hope, as our knowledge increases, new frameworks will develop and the guidelines offered here will be added to, enriched, or developed in yet unknown ways – or become obsolete.

THE SOCIAL SIGNIFICANCE OF MEDITATION

I started this book by pointing out that the real goal of meditation was to 'come home' to parts of ourself that we had lost, to become fuller human beings. Surely we meditate in order to gain serenity, peace, joy, greater efficiency in everyday life, to increase our power to love, to achieve a deeper view of reality. These are the goals we start with, and they are good and realistic goals for this discipline and for ourselves. Our real goal, however, is to become more complete, to more fully live the potential of being human.

All of us know, at one level or another, how little we have fulfilled ourselves, how much of our potential has been left untrained and underdeveloped. We have seen ourselves and the rest of the human race, in moments of greatness, standing tall and beautiful. We have seen how most of our lives are lived far below this level and the ways our crippled and stunted personalities have brought forth in us narrowness, insensitivity, meanness, stupidity and self-destructive activities, leading to pain and death for ourselves and the others.

We have all seen ourselves and the rest of our species act as angels to each other and as wolves to each other.

It may well be that much of our crippling is due to the loss of that part of ourselves that we strive to regain through meditation, through following the mystic's path to the fuller completion of ourselves and thus the fuller completion of our relationship with others and with our home, the universe. All three go together. We cannot be more complete in one respect of our being without being more complete in the others. Being stunted in one set of these relationships inevitably means a stunting in the others.

Let us explore some aspects of this incompleteness we live and some of its implications. Suppose we start with the strange and dramatic world of the paranormal abilities, of telepathy, clairvoyance, precognition, the whole range of occurrences we label as ESP, Extra Sensory Perception. What can we say today about the nature of man and the paranormal?

There are certain things we can say. We can say that if the paranormal ability exists in a few of us, it exists – in varying degrees, perhaps – in all of us, that it is part of our nature, part of being human. Except in those situations in which special pathology is operating, as in colour blindness, what exists potentially in one person exists potentially to some degree in all persons. We can say that if it exists and is not potentiated, does not surface and demonstrate its existence, we are repressing part of ourselves.

We can see the widespread nature of this repression by the fact that ESP can be trained to appear – as the 'Home Circles' trained so many individuals in the first part of the century – by the fact that it is more frequent in some cultures than others and that within a culture the amount of ESP showing varies in different cultural periods.

Recently, as part of a research programme, I set up training seminars in a specific paranormal ability. The majority of the individuals participating had never had a psychic experience in their lives. The channel was apparently closed or nonexistent. About eight out of ten of them were able to learn the ability to a functionally useful level.

The importance of ESP occurrences is not in the phenomena themselves. To focus on these directly is to miss the main point. Their importance is that they clearly indicate the existence of another part of our being, of a part of our potential for existence and relationship. This part we must develop to achieve our full humanness; we leave it undeveloped only at heavy cost.

From our experience in psychiatry and psychology, we can unequivocally say that there is a price tag that must be paid if we repress a major part of our being. The price tag is a loss of joy and zest. The price tag is anxiety and aggression; it is hate and rejection of the self and hate and suspicion of others. We know – from long years of psychotherapeutic exploration – that a part of the self cannot be rejected, cannot be unaccepted and unlived without paying this price. Today we can say more than this also. We can say *what* is repressed. It is not just paranormal ability, but that part of us, that way of being in the cosmos, which makes the paranormal possible. It is a half of our being. We are speaking of a part of man that must live and perceive and react and *be* in the universe in a different way, a different mode from our ordinary way. It is the way of the *One* rather than the way of the *Many*. It is the way in which we know we are all a part of one another and a part of the cosmos and that our separation, our alienation from each other, is illusion.

It is this potential for being in the world in a different way that the mystics insist is a part of man and is almost always unfulfilled. For reasons of biological survival we must learn to live in the everyday world of the many, the world of identity and separateness. This half of our being we are trained to express, but modern living tends to repress the other half which then withers in undernourishment. It is to the gardening of the unexpressed half that the mystic devotes his long and arduous training. And, as his ability to use this part develops, he claims he perceives the world in that way, a way in which he is no longer separate and cut off, no longer alone, but is an integral and inseparable part of the total *Gestalt*, the total One that makes up the cosmos.

My first introduction to this strange view – the world of the One – came when I was investigating the great sensitives. A 'sensitive' is a person who, far more often than the rest of us, demonstrates the paranormal acquisition of knowledge, who has information he could not possibly have acquired from the senses or from extrapolation of previously known information. A 'great sensitive' is one who not only has this ability to a very outstanding degree, but who has also been extensively studied by experts in this field, studied in the laboratory and in everyday life, and about whom there is not the faintest smell of chicanery. When I asked these sensitives, 'How does the world look at the moment you are receiving this paranormally acquired information?' they replied that it looked very different than at other, ordinary moments. And after long study and enquiry with them, I began to understand this other world view, this new, strange, alien, but somehow familiar and homelike, way of conceptualizing and being in the world which they described. It was indeed a different world. The most important aspects of a person or a thing concerned relationships, not identity. It was the being part of the whole, a subfield of the great harmonies and energies of the cosmos, that was the salient and crucial aspect, not the specific identity defined by how it was cut off and separate from the rest of reality. Indeed, individuality and uniqueness were secondary to oneness and relatedness, secondary and almost illusory. All things, events, entities, objects flowed into one another and could not be meaningfully separated from each other. Space connected objects rather than separated them. Time flowed as a seamless garment, and past, present and future were arbitrary illusions. From this view all actions and events were part of a harmony; the hawk, the swoop and the hare were one. Since nothing could be separated from the total being of the universe, nothing could be characterized as 'good' or 'evil' since this would mean so characterizing the total cosmos, which is far above this sort of labelling. The best way to gain information was not through the senses, those 'blind guides to illusion', but through knowing that spectator and spectacle were one and that there is no bar to information flowing within that one, that nothing comes between a thing and itself. It was this way that the sensitives said they regarded the world at the moments when they were acquiring information paranormally.

The description was exactly the same as the way the mystics regarded the world when their training began to take effect. The mystics of the East and West, of the classical, medieval and modern periods, were in complete agreement on this.

A third group also regarded the world as being put together in exactly the same way. The Einsteinian physicists described the structure of the world in identical terms: the three sets of description – medium, mystic and physicist – are isomorphic; they cannot be differentiated from each other meaningfully although the starting points, techniques, attitudes and goals of the three are quite different.[1]

All three groups achieve their goals: the sensitive with his evidence of paranormally acquired information; the mystic with his serenity, peace and joy, and the capacity for effective action he achieves; the physicist with his control of nature. So the new, strange view of reality appears to be a valid one, as valid as the everyday view we hold, no more, no less.

The real importance of the paranormal is that it shows and demonstrates the existence of another part of man's nature, another aspect of his potential being, an aspect long hidden in the mists of art, legend, myth, magic and mystery that our explorers of reality are now bringing to the light.

We know the price of the repression of part of our being. We need both aspects, not just one. Every serious mystical school has insisted that one without the other leaves man stunted and unfulfilled.

If we need both and are potentially both, why do we not have both? Perhaps the major reason is that our normal, everyday world view not only has biological survival value – both for the individual and the species – but it is also complex and difficult to learn. The first twenty years or so of our life must be spent in learning how to operate in the world of the many. (Perhaps someday we will learn how to do this and *at the same time* nourish the other half of our being, but, except in rare individual cases, it has never been done.) This is reflected in the old view in India of how a man should design his life: the first twenty years as a youth, the second twenty as a worker and head of a household, the third twenty as a student of the One and a gardener of this part of himself. The fourth twenty years are spent as a teacher to guide other students.

We can see this as a facet of a development sequence we have largely neglected and are now beginning to understand, and whose implications we have never plumbed. It is a concept that human life is organically divided into parts in terms of our orientation toward reality and that this has tremendous implications for all aspects of our life.

In the first half of our lives we must learn the terribly hard task of learning to function in the world of the many and functioning effectively in it. Our survival rests on this. Knowing of, and cultivating the other half of our being as we go, we first learn the path of the many and then act with strength, will and effectiveness in it. The second half of our lives we repeat the process with the emphasis reversed. Then we learn how to function with the perception and being of the world of the One and then function effectively in it, combining both aspects as a teacher. We see one aspect of the steps in this developmental sequence in Carl Jung's statement that he had never seen a patient over thirty-five whose problem was not basically a religious one and who was not cured when his religious problem was solved. This corresponds well to the Indian idea of changing your whole style of life at age forty.

In another place Jung speaks of the second adolescence that some people go through, usually between the ages of thirty-five and fifty. In this they turn in their basic orientation to life from concern with the opinions of others to concern with the being and growth of the self. Jung speaks of those who go through this second adolescence as the fortunate ones and has compassion for those who do not.

From my own experience as a psychologist in a hospital with a very large percentage of dying patients, I can bear this out. Those who had made the change could use me as a friend or as a liaison person with the rest of the hospital staff, but they did not need me as a psychotherapist. They faced their deaths with strength and confidence. Those who had not made the change were quite different. They were full of fears and regrets. One such patient told her physician, 'You don't understand, Doctor. I am not crying because I am going to die. I am crying because I have never lived.'

One of the clearest signs of this change comes with a painful symptom that has been little understood. This is the forgetting of recent details that individuals in their sixties and seventies frequently start to experience. The petty minutiae of everyday life tend to be rapidly lost from memory. Regarded as the loss of an ability, this has proven very painful to many people. What do we know about this symptom? We know it is not basically organic, that when the present becomes again fully exciting and involving – as when a new profession or interest is entered into with zest – the symptoms largely disappears. We know that memories of the past remain clear; it is the memories of the present that go.

Let us look at this symptom as a sign of an ignored developmental sequence. By sixty the individual has long since gone past the natural time to turn to cultivating the other half of himself. Developmentally, however, he is overready to turn his mind to the general, to relationships rather than details. It is necessary in the first forty to fifty years to remember details accurately and effectively; we are concerned with tasks and vocations that demand this. 'What size transistor fits here?' 'What are the legal precedents for that?' 'What are the psychological variables involved here?' 'What groceries are needed today?' we remember these effectively. It is the developmental time for these concerns. 'For everything under the sun there is a season . . . ' Now, however, as life reaches the halfway point, a new orientation begins to appear and, unless it is gardened, in its blocked force it blocks also the effectiveness of our previous orientation. We turn naturally here to the general, the relationships, the upper end of the spectrum. We see with the artist's eye that sees meaning and relationship first, rather than with the mechanic's and administrator's eye that sees identities first. I have questioned many people who complain of this 'forgetting' symptom. They have great trouble remembering the name to go with a face they have met recently. They are always surprised when they realize that they do not forget the emotional tone between them and that person at the time that they met. They remember the relationship and its meaning; they forget the details. Their eye and orientation have changed, but because they do not understand that this is part of their development and a sign to go forward, they regard it as a loss and so it becomes one. I have never known of a mystic or a sensitive of any age with this symptom. We ignore our human developmental patterns at our peril.

It is, of course, not only in the last half of our life that the One, the Universal part of us is important. We are all our lives a special species; we live *sub species aeternitis*, under the roof of eternity. It is the large things that give our life the *meaning* it must have, not the details and mechanics of life. Without vision, without meaning, our lives decay, and we feel the possibility of ego and bodily disintegration and discoherence. The large things – laughter, love, religious awe, beauty – can only be understood by accepting the validity of this part of our being. They can never be understood by an analysis, be it Freudian or behaviouristic, that ignores it.

The meaning and validity of our lives are given by that part of us that relates to the world of the One. The mechanics and techniques by means of which we live our lives are given by that part of us that relates to the world of the Many. It is the One that gives meaning to the Many, and the Many that gives form to the One. It is relationships that make identity real and meaningful, as it is identity that makes relationships possible. It is only when we have access to both parts of our being that we can remember the meaning of our own existence.

If we accent and live both of our ways of being in the world, then we know truly that our lives have meaning and validity, that no man is an island, each is a part of the main. If we just live in the world of multiplicity, then we are forced to the conclusion, in Alfred Noyes's words, that 'we are each of us an island and each of us alone, in the land where the dead dreams go.'

This part of us relates to our connectedness and to our real relationships not only with others, but with the universe as a whole. To the degree it is expressed and lived, we feel with Giordano Bruno that 'out of this world we cannot fall'. To the degree it is not accepted and lived, we feel with Pascal that 'the emptiness of the infinite spaces frightens me.' This loss of connectedness, stemming from a lack of acceptance and nourishing of this part of us, weakens our sense of identity. Our sense of identity needs relationships: it is terribly weakened and collapses without them. A schizophrenic girl said as her husband left the hospital after a visit, 'Now I no longer know who I am. I will know again when he returns.' Kurt Goldstein put it, 'It is not right to say we have a self. The self is never isolated.' The more cut off we are by the repression of this part of us, the more vulnerable we feel. Our cut-off state begets anxiety. Our anxieties beget hostility.

One very common but disastrous way we solve both is by forming into groups with a common enemy. In this way when we feel too alone, too vulnerable, too meaningless, we find or design a situation in which we have comrades who need us and relate to us, an enemy to discharge our hostility on, a purpose in life to destroy that enemy. Even when we feel safe for the moment, we prepare for the alienated times. In Saul Alinsky's phrase, 'we keep a fight in the bank'. All of us know the meaning of the cynical sentence 'Friends are acquaintances who have the same enemies.'

Further, when we do not live this other side of ourselves, we lose part of the greatest of the ethical and behavioural guidelines of our race. If I know that you and I are part of one another and, in this, part of the whole, the One, then I treat you as I treat myself. And I treat myself well, tenderly and carefully, since I know that I am a part of something so tremendous, so great, that, if for this reason only, it is holy.

If I do not know that we are also One, then I see only our cut-off and isolated qualities. I treat you differently than I do myself. I have not nourished that part of myself that knows the answer to Cain's question, the answer that says, 'We are each our brother's keepers because we are each our brothers.' Every great religion and religious idea stem from this point.

Our perception of the way of the One brings with it the knowledge also of the deep meaning of ourselves and the cosmos. 'Where does God dwell?' 'Wherever man lets him in,' goes the Hasidic statement. We *know* what Suzuki Roshi meant when he said, 'All is God and there is no God'; what John Donne meant when he said, 'God is a stone in a stone, an angel in an angel and a straw in a straw'; and the meaning of the sentence 'All things contain the indwelling light.' 'No place is empty of Him,' says the Talmud. I have never known anyone who has learned to live this part of themselves who has feared death or thought it was the end.

Our lack of openness of this channel of perception increases our loneliness and anxiety. This, in turn, helps close the channel further as we try to buttress our safety and end our loneliness with power and/or material wealth; it is an attempt that, since it does not respond to our real human need -- to express this other part of ourselves – can never be satisfied. It can only extend itself in a vain, endless race for *more* power, *more* material goods, in the hope that somehow, sometime, enough power, enough wealth, will ease our pain and fear.

What can we say about the nature of man from all this? We look around us; we read our history and see a mixed being, neither angel nor demon. He is killer and healer, seeking sometimes the best and sometimes the worst for himself and for others. Pope in his 'Essay on Man' put it this way:

Born on this Isthmus of a middle state
A being darkly wise and widely great
He hangs between; in doubt to act or rest
In doubt to deem himself a God or beast,
In doubt his mind or body to prefer,
Born but to die and reasoning but to err,
Sole judge of truth in endless error hurled
The glory, jest and riddle of the world.

It is interesting to note how we indicate our awareness of the need for both parts of the words we use: 'clever,' 'intelligent,' 'wise,' 'Clever' means the ability to deal quickly and effectively and ingeniously with one aspect of the world of multiplicity. 'Intelligent' means the ability to deal with the entire world of multiplicity. 'Wise' means the fusion of both words, the functioning in both, the complete person. Here stand the acknowledged greatest of our race, Socrates and Jesus, the Buddha and Lao-tzu. 'Render unto God that which belongs to God and unto Caesar that which belongs to

Caesar' is a much more profound statement than is generally realized.

How much of this mixed quality is related to repression of a major part of man's being and the loss of a major source of his relatedness and at-homeness in the world? As we look at the mystics – those who by long training and work have recovered this part of themselves – we see serenity, peace, joy, a lack of anxiety and hostility, a quality to their lives that is almost blinding and deeply inspiring to those who observe them. Those who knew the Baal Shem Tov or Saint Teresa or Ramakrishna, or the others like them, plainly felt that these mystics were more completely human than the rest of us. The mystics have no need to identify themselves with national units or with races. They have no need for enemies to hate. They are nice people to share the planet with.

In a mystical or peak experience, or when we are fully centred and together, whose world is so lacking in colour that he needs drugs to sharpen his existence? Who – since his anxieties and vulnerabilities are so much lessened – feels the need to fortify himself with power trips or material goals, or other doomed-to-fail security systems? Who does not feel so good and open that he understands the meaning of the statement of Rumi, 'Love is the astrolabe of the mysteries of God'?

One of the most frightening things today is the behaviour of the esoteric schools of mystical training. For centuries, many of them have been hidden and underground. If you wished training it would, for many of them, take you three to five years to locate one and another few years to gain admission. To work with a Sufi teacher, for example, would take at least that long. Today nearly all such schools have surfaced and are actively seeking new students. Serious Sufi teachers advertise in the newspapers. All have the same explanation. They say, in effect, 'If our carefully hoarded knowledge is not used now, it will be too late. There is not more time, it is now or never for the human race to change, to become mature, to find and live the unused side of itself.'

And until we recover this almost lost part of us and live it, our other endeavours shall not succeed in their hidden goal of fulfilling us. Thomas Merton put it, 'What can we gain by sailing to the moon if we are not able to cross the abyss that separates us from ourselves?'

We have a great drive, a need to grow, to become more. This is what Pir Vilayat Khan meant when he said, 'No force anywhere on earth is as imperialistic as the human soul. It occupies and is occupied in turn, but it always considers its empire too narrow. Suffocating, it desires to conquer the world in order to breathe.'

The blocked energy of this drive to *be*, to potentiate ourselves, is awesome in its strength and is one of the factors that makes it hard for us to stop killing each other, that seems to keep driving us down the road to extinction. Without the other half of ourselves we are crippled, stunted beings. Only complete can we live with ourselves and others as full human beings. The answer lies in working both outside and inside. Either half by itself is not enough. We *must* work for social good and against injustice and pain. The everyday world of multiplicity is half of our nature and we must act effectively and strongly in it. But it is not enough by itself. We must also find and garden that which is inside. 'The kingdom of Heaven lies within you,' wrote one great mystic. And Omar the Tentmaker wrote that *both* heaven and hell lie within each of us.

It has never succeeded before that the vision of the complete man, the mystical insight, has worked for more than a few. It has never changed the multitude to the degree that is necessary now. The teachings of the Lamb of God led to the Inquisition; followers of the Lord Buddha and of Mohammed enjoy killing each other. This time we cannot afford to have another failure. There is opportunity now in the great public interest in mysticism and meditation, and we must use and encourage this interest and need to the fullest. But we must be aware of the past failures lest we repeat them. Perhaps if we can combine the new knowledge we have from psychology and psychiatry with the old knowledge of the mystical training schools, we can bring the possibility of a more mature and complete race into being. We have very much to learn and to do and the time is short. But this is not a cause for discouragement, but for excitement over the chance we have and full effort to use it. Let us not repeat, by our actions, the famous words, 'It has never been done and it can't be done. I told Wilbur and I told Orville and I'm telling you. It can't be done.'

One thing is clear. It is only as we garden ourselves and each other toward our fullest humanhood that we can come to know how at home we are in the universe and that this is a good world for man. And to know the meaning of the Haiku that Nikos Kazantzakis put into the mouth of Saint Francis of Assisi:

I said to the almond tree,
'Sister, speak to me of God,'
And the almond tree blossomed.

AFTERWORD

When asked to write an afterword to this book of Dr LeShan's I was immediately engaged in asking myself what purpose such an afterword could serve for a book that is already so courageous, so challenging and so complete?

After pondering the question is seemed obvious that its only function would be to set what came before in a broader context, so that the significance of Dr LeShan's contribution to the literature on meditation might be appreciated more fully and explored more profoundly.

In the ancient tradition of the spiritual guide, I have shared in the development of this book as the one who on occasion asked the questions that needed to be asked and challenged the thought process when it bogged down. Now, if I may, I would like to create a setting within which the facets of Dr LeShan's thought and experience can shine with the radiance that might be obscured by the combination of his modesty and scientific caution.

A constellation of recent research has thrown light on the nature of man as a creature capable of creative thought about himself and his place in the universe. This research has in varied ways indicated that the nature of meditation is to isolate resources and develop skills in the use of psychic energy.

Some of this research moves beyond the confines of the laboratory and focuses on human experience that cannot be driven into a small corner. Jerome Frank says, 'No less than the "English scientists" Jeans and Eddington, Planck and Einstein are "romantics". Their assertions rest not on knowledge but on faith.'¹ So it is in the company of the great scientists that one looks at life not in the narrow confines of the tested formulae but in the more heroic speculations concerning the phenomena of man and his experience.

Meditation is achieved at the point where mind and spirit converge. The mind is the instrument that disciplines, and the spirit represents the special endowment of man that must be cultivated by special control and dedicated efforts. It is important, then, that we seek to clarify the resources of being that we would bring together in the creative processes of meditation.

What is the mind? How does it work? What is it we do with the mind in meditation?

Basic to any productive enquiry is the scientist's concept of his own mind and its products, meaning and value. Yet the more the products of the mind have been evaluated, the more difficult it has become to explain them on the basis of the processes observed. For the mind is always so much more than the brain that the relationship bespeaks a mystery of profound proportions. Nowhere are the words of Harris Elliot Kirk more germane than in the knowledge of the mind. 'As knowledge advances, as the secrets of nature are explored and revealed, the more aware are we that we live in a mysterious universe.'²

The physiologist and the psychoanalyst offer quite different though perhaps supplementary concepts of the mind's life. Yet both point in the direction of those mysterious qualities that would relate this knowing instrument to sources of knowledge that cannot be explained either by DNA, body chemistry or psychological insight.

Lord Adrian, a Nobel Prize-winning physiologist, gives a description of the mind as an energy-creating instrument of profound complexity.

There are about ten thousand million nerve cells in the brain, and they are connected by an interlacing network of threads so that a cell is rarely active without influencing its neighbours. The essential activity seems to consist in a sudden change in the cell surface which allows a momentary escape of some of the molecules. This surface change can be repeated at very short intervals so that the cell may become active and inactive as often as fifty times a second, and each time it becomes active an impulse will pass out from the cell to its neighbours or farther afield to other parts of the central nervous system . . . Whenever nerve cells or fibres are active, they produce electrical effects – rapid changes of potential corresponding to the changes in surface membranes. The electrical charges are very small, and they can only be detected by placing electrodes in contact with the cells or with the fluids and tissues close to them, but nowadays it is a simple matter to amplify them until they are large enough to be recorded photographically . . . Records of these electrical charges show that the messages which are sent into the brain from the sense organs are made up of repeated impulses in the nerve fibres . . . so when we see a light or hear a sound, the first thing that happens in the brain is the arrival of a great many nerve impulses. [3]

Lord Adrian says that 'ordinary casual thinking does not involve widespread changes in cell activity,'[4] but that intense meditation, concentration or stress thinking produces the cell activity that increases the production of electrical energy in the brain. This concept of the brain makes it responsive to the laws governing the behaviour of particles. It could be that revelation and the phenomena of telepathy are part of this particle behaviour. Certainly meditation is a form of concentration that heightens specific forms of sensitivity.

The psychoanalytic approach to the functioning of the brain and the products of mental activity caution us to relate this phenomenon to those endowments and experiences that could reasonably explain it. Modern scientific research has done much to throw light on the processes which have traditionally led to a belief in revealed knowledge. This does not mean that there is no such knowledge, but it does mean that much that was formerly attributed to such sources will have to be re-evaluated and screened to make proper allowance for our new understanding of the structure of personality and the influence of lower levels of consciousness on behaviour. This in turn would make it possible for us to examine both the mentally disturbed and the mystic to properly attribute the observed phenomena to their proper source. Only then will we bring into sharp focus the unique quality of the knowledge that comes from directly revealed sources.

Let us fix clearly in our minds what the traditional idea of revelation is. There has long been a feeling that man has a capacity of consciousness for direct communication with cosmic wisdom. In his *Institutes* John Calvin claimed that there was a *sensus divinitatis* deep in every human mind which is the source of revelation supported by the proofs of the world of natural phenomena.[5] Schleiermacher carries this idea one step further through what he considers to be a *mysterium tremendum*, a heightened consciousness that adds to speculative reason the powerful insights that are rooted in feelings.

John Caird tried to bridge the gap between the idea of revelation as a capacity of mind in contrast to an overflow of feeling by claiming that truth is universal, whether natural or revealed. 'Revealed truth cannot belong to a different order from all other truth that appeals to the human consciousness . . . On the contrary, by universal admission the teaching of revelation finds its best and only sufficient evidence in the consciousness of the believer.'[6] This consciousness causes a unity of being that is not divisible into thought and feeling. But in meditation strong feeling can be a stimulus of mental activity and disciplined mental activity can capitalize on strong emotions.

The idea of revelation is based on the premise that the mind of man is not only able to be aware of cosmic knowledge, but also that in some mysterious way there seems to be a cosmic initiative seeking to make itself known to man. This calls for the mind that is not only seeking but also willing to be sought. This is apparently why some mystics engage in an alternation between contemplation and meditation. John Baille implies this when he writes, 'The knowing mind is active in attending, selecting and interpreting; but it must attend to, select from and interpret what is presented to it; and, therefore, it must be passive as well as active.'[7]

The knowing mind is finite, and in its functioning is usually limited by the structure of symbolization that serves as the equipment of communication. We use language to transmit ideas. The language is not the idea, but is the conscious effort to make the idea tangible.

The artist uses canvas and colour to speak his deeper insights. He feels that the communication has somehow lost its power if it has to be explained in words. The composer uses sound to transmit thought and feeling and again feels that any effort to put it into words dims the deeper meaning. The mystic employs silence as a form of communication charge with meaning. So Quakers in centering down and using creative silence employ a rich form of spiritual language. In meditation something of the creative nature of the being achieves a meaning that is not bound by the symbolic structure of language. The forms this creative process employ vary with our understanding of the nature of the cosmos and the nature of the human personality.

Science finds itself in a dilemma concerning the knowing instrument. All of the processes of science ultimately depend upon a faith in the validity of the mind's functioning, but the scientific method cannot be employed to establish the validity of its own products. Charles S. Sherrington, a physiologist, states the impasse in these words, 'Thoughts and feelings are not amenable to the matter concept. They lie outside it. Mind goes, therefore, in our spatial world more ghostly than a ghost, invisible, intangible; it is a thing not even of outline; it is not a thing but remains without sensual confirmation.'[8]

Thus the revelation associated with the meditative response has a validity of its own that cannot be questioned, although reasonable efforts may be made to bring it into conformity with other aspects of what we call reality. What the physiologist is aware of is also the dilemma of the psychologist. Fritz Kunz sums up the question in this way:

A really decisive issue is now before us: Albert Einstein, Max Planck, A.H.Compton, J.C.Maxwell and others have demonstrated the reality of something known to exist, and easily demonstrated, but which is quite beyond direct reach of the senses. If something real, yet quite non-material, can exist outside of us, are we not permitted to suppose that non-material, but forceful reality – mind, for example – may exist inside of us? In man, is brain an instrument of more than sensation and response?[9]

Science may ask the questions in a way that sharpens up the process by which the thinker uses his thinking instrument, but such questions do not become a final evaluation of the processes involved. Here the quality of being achieves a meaning equal to more than the sum of the parts. As the scientific approach to the human body reveals a principle or resonance at work between the body and the spiritual nature that inhabits it, so the study of the brain-mind relationship reveals a validity for belief in a creative responsiveness between the Intelligence within the individual and an Intelligence beyond the individual that cannot be verified or denied by scientific methods or instruments. However, the very life of science as well as the achievements of the spiritual being are bound up with a faith that trusts and employs the processes by which knowledge, wisdom and revelation are amalgamated into a high form of human experience, the creative faith. Science states the thesis concerning the plus factor in the nature of human life. Something beyond the scientific method must be employed to make this plus factor an operative reality in human experience. This important task is implicit in Dr LeShan's concept of mind and meditation.

But Dr LeShan does not stop there. He has the courage to move on into even more rarefied climates, yet always with the scientist's caution. Like Heraclitus, who developed a theory of the spirit as the principle governing all happenings, Dr LeShan confronts the therapeutic and ethical implications of meditation. Here he moves into the realm of the spirit. If mind is the source of disciplined meditation, and the spirit is the endowment for disciplining, we must ask, what do we really know about this force or quality of being we call spiritual?

The unique quality of man's nature has always been a matter of deep concern to him. Self-consciousness is not only a privilege but is also a burden. Students of anthropology interpret many of the early rites and customs of primitive tribes as efforts to deal with this problem of a spiritual nature. Through the long history of man's emergence as a civilized being, he has attempted various solutions to the problem of his spiritual nature. He has at one time made it paramount in his life and at other times denied its existence.

Many centuries ago Saint Augustine looked deep within himself to find an intuitive answer to the problem of his spiritual nature.

The personhood of man, therefore, is an interinvolvement of rich inter-communication or dialogue. Man, though he feels lonely, is always in encounter with himself. The more he presses this dialogue of the self, the deeper he goes into the self itself. Sooner or later he encounters the Totally Other within the self. This is a radical departure from the sharp cleavage between the subjective and the objective world which one finds in classical idealism. There is an inner reality which is as surely objective as any outer reality.[10]

In his own words he says,

Don't go outside yourself, return into yourself. The dwelling place of truth is in the inner man. And if you discover your own nature as subject to change, then go beyond that nature. But, remember that, when you thus go beyond it, it is the reasoning soul which you go beyond. Press on, therefore, toward the source from which the light of reason itself is kindled.[11]

So the spirit of man is a deep inner divine pattern or image that is seeking to emerge, and while the problems of emergence may involve struggle, they are struggles that grow out of a totality of being, and not of diverse natures in conflict within the being. In fact, the precise exercises Dr LeShan suggests help to achieve this inner unification as the launching pad for spiritual achievement.

This creative spiritual quality Leonard Cottrell considers to be essential to interpersonal competence.

> *The component is perhaps the least amenable to precise definition and division into manageable variables which can be measured. It is ironical that the so-called tough-minded scientists and hard-headed practical people are inclined to look askance at this category as a proper object of scientific study, and yet all of these people demand appraisals of this quality in prospective associates on whom heavy responsibility for leadership and initiative will fall.* [12]

This is a borderline quality that leads toward a spiritual concept. Peter Berger, a sociologist, explores it further in his book *A Rumor of Angels, or The Rediscovery of the Supernatural*.

The validity of the assumption about the creative spiritual nature of man is attested by David Riesman in his judgment of Freud's attitude toward religious thinking.

> *Religion can tell us a good deal about the individual believer and the social system in which he exists. We can, in socio-psychological terms, interpret the part religion plays in the life of men and groups. But this part is seldom simple and monolithic. Paradoxically, Freud seems to have taken too much at face value the religious opposition to science, and failed to see, at least in this particular, that we have not said the last word about a man's rationality when we have stamped him as a believer – his religion may be the very sign of his rationality . . .* [13]

Freud's basic pessimism about human nature may have prevented him from ever having a healthy judgment of man's spiritual response to life.

Jung and Sorokin moved a long step beyond these tentative and cautious assertions of Riesman. Sorokin asserts that the mechanistic and materialistic view of personality tries to limit spirit by biology, while the spiritual view of personality seeks to understand mind in its relation to the energy sources in the cosmos and thereby gives mind cosmic significance, purpose and meaning. 'The biological unconscious lies below the level of the conscious energies and the superconscious (genius, creative elan, the extra-sensory, the divine inspiration, supra-conscious intuition, etc.) lies above the level of any conscious, rational and logical thought of energy.'[14]

The more daring minds in the personality sciences are willing to organize their systems of thought to make room for this spiritual element. Sorokin speaks of the 'Idealistic', Berdyaev projects a 'New Medieval' with its spiritual emphasis; Spengler outlines the culture of a 'New Religiosity' and Toynbee writes of a 'New Universal Church'. VonDomasus says the whole sweep of anthropology is toward the highest level of life conceivable, 'The religious man,' and Pierre Teilhard de Chardin centres his concept of evolution on the energy of creation that is moving man toward a spiritual state of being. Erich Fromm looks deeply into the thought of the humanist prophets of ancient Israel and sees the validity of an inner hope and writes, 'You Shall Be as Gods.' It is in this daring tradition that Dr LeShan looks deeply into the needs of men in a fractured and fracturing moment in history and sees the validity of the inner processes that can help man discover his supreme identity through the disciplines and fruits of meditation.

One philosopher looking at this historical moment sees a trend among both young and old that is moving from 'predominantly materialistic, egoistic, hedonistic, utilitarian, mechanistic and cerebrally-rational to dominantly idealistic, spiritual, altruistic, organic and supra-conscious or intuitional' ideas of the human soul.[15] It may be that Dr LeShan's concept of the moral responsibility basic to creative meditation can serve as a valid antidote to the trend toward sociopathic and psychopathic acting out of meaninglessness. Even though social thinkers have been more reserved in expressing their thoughts than the physical and biological scientists, they have felt the impact of such thought and hopefully adjust their social theories in accordance with this new trend toward a spiritual interpretation of life and human organization.

What man has been sensitive to through long history is now hesitatingly recognized by the social services, clearly affirmed in specialized branches of psychological research, and presented as a possibility in the physical sciences. No less a scientist than Heisenberg writes,

> *The concepts 'soul' or 'life' do not occur in atomic physics, and they could not, even indirectly, be derived as complicated consequences of some natural law. Their existence certainly does not indicate the presence of any fundamental substance other than energy, but it shows only the action of other kinds of forms which we cannot match with the mathematical forms of modern atomic physics . . . If we want to describe living or mental processes, we shall have to abandon these structures. It may be that we shall have to introduce yet other concepts.*[16]

So the soul theory, the special place for the spirit of man, emerges into a new pattern of thought, verified and verifiable, not by the exact sciences, but not in opposition to them. Much of science now seems united in the strong feeling that there is a primary place for spiritual quality in all of life. The concept of the spirit that emerges from scientific enquiry is different in degree but not in nature from that of mystical thought. Science can go only so far in showing what this spiritual quality is. The mystics' inclination is more concerned with employing this spiritual energy in the process of living.

Jung in his psychoanalytic studies found that there was a quest among his patients for a spiritual meaning for life. Science now affirms that there is justification for such a quest, and though the scientific method cannot go all the way, it can point directions toward a reasonable framework within which the quest may be made. Years ago Alfred Steinmetz said that the great discoveries of the twentieth century would be in the realm of the spirit. It looks as though science is making a major contribution to this search for spiritual meaning.

It may seem strange to hear a biologist speak like a mystic, yet Edmund Sinnott wrote,

All this, the theologian says, is simply to admit that man is a child of God, made spiritually in His image and with a divine spark in his heart. What we have called the human spirit, he continues, risen from simple biological purposiveness, is much more than meaningless emotion and may legitimately be regarded as an intermediary between the material and the Divine. Such a concept will startle the biologist, but it should reassure the man of faith by providing a reasonable means, through the aspiring, purposive nature of life itself, for a contact between man and God. Some would prefer to believe that the divine in man was planted in him by the Deity, and others that it developed during the upward course of evolution. The important point is that man's spirit, certainly an inhabitant of his living, material body, may without philosophical impropriety be regarded as similar in nature to a far greater Spirit, in which thus, literally, he may be said to live and move and have his being.[17]

In the scientifc insights that point a direction toward man's unfulfilled but potential nature we see a valid reason for the disciplines of the meditator. In his quest for cosmic meaning for his special endowment, he is not apt to be satisfied until that vague image becomes the mystery-penetrating, wonder-inspiring and purpose-revealing essence of existence.

Man is constantly immersed in three force fields, and he could not live without their impact on his being. While they differ widely in nature they are not in conflict at the point where his living spirit integrates them. Cosmic radiation, electromagnetic and gravitational forcefields are constantly at work on life. Man does not need to understand their working to benefit from their action on his being. In a singular and perhaps more rarefied way he is resonant to a psychic forcefield that interacts with his finite nature and the timeless elements at work in the universe with which he is essentially one. It is toward the meaning of this unity that the mystic seeks the integration of his being. The discipline of meditation is employed for that purpose.

How does the meditative process contribute to the sense of cosmic unity and supreme identification? In his integration of experience the mystic denies the appearance of conflict or diversity in ultimate reality. The more practical-minded have always challenged the mystic with the problems of good and evil, the false and the true, the beautiful and the ugly with their apparent conflicts. But the mystic finds the answer in a spiritual experience exalted enough to resolve all the differences in a higher unity. The mood of scientific enquiry is more friendly to this idea now than it has ever been before just because what is seen and what is not seen, what is experienced and what is beyond experience in the ordinary sensory meaning of the word, has now come to share a working unity. What the scientist knows and does not know, what he sees and cannot see, are made up of the same mystery and all clues indicate that they share a common quality. How much this sounds like the intuitive judgment of Parmenides, who claimed that reality is one and indivisible, and Heraclitus, who said, 'We step and do not step in the same river, we are and are not.' Such unity is the achievement of the meditator in response to the creative spirit he discovers within himself. The growing mysticism of science is a comparable response to the creative, contemplating spirit. And the creative, contemplating spirit comes alive in the person doing the hard work of disciplined mediation.

Can there then be a metaphysics of mediation? Can there be a philosophy adequate to explain the phenomena we observe and the goals we seek? Bertrand Russell saw the problem clearly. 'Metaphysics . . . has been developed, from the first, by the union and conflict of two very different human impulses, the one urging men toward mysticism, and the other urging men toward science.'[18] This conflict can be resolved not by science or religion, but by a philosophical effort to find an adequate basis for viewing all of man and his experience. He continued, 'But the greatest men who have been philosophers have felt the need both of science and of mysticism: the attempt to harmonize the two was what made their life, and what always must, for all its arduous uncertainty, make philosophy, to some minds, a greater thing than either science or religion.'[19] It is the effort to discover a philosophical base and a metaphysical formula for meditation that can be adequate and valid that may be the most significant contribution of Dr LeShan to the literature on meditation.

Meditation as the fusion of a disciplined mind and the creative spirit is rooted in a compelling faith. A good case could be made for the fact that the faith of the scientist in the capacity of his own mind to know truth is itself a mystical experience. Plato saw that this was a basic problem of science. The problem is still basic. The ideas of Tillich and Einstein could be interchanged at this point. Einstein said,

> Science can only be created by those who are thoroughly imbued with the aspirations toward truth and understanding. This source of feeling, however, springs from the sphere of religion. To this there also belongs the faith in the possibility that the regulations valid for the world of existence are rational; that is, comprehensible to reason. I cannot conceive of a genuine scientist without that profound faith. The situation may be expressed by an image: Science without religion is lame, religion without science is blind.[20]

In the spirit Tillich says,

> There is no conflict between faith in its true nature and reason in its true nature. This includes the assertion that there is no essential conflict between faith and the cognitive function of reason . . . Therefore, it is a very poor method of defending the truth of faith against the truth of science, if theologians point to the preliminary character of every scientific statement in order to provide a place of retreat from the truth of faith.[21]

So the cognitive process and the faith employed in the use of it stand as the valid expressions of a mystical response so basic to life that the answers are found in life rather than in either science or religion.

Certainly, in his approach to a major experience of life affirmation, Dr LeShan seeks no place for safe retreat. Rather, he carries on the work of his friend Abraham Maslow, who broke new trails in finding the way to heightened sensitivity and personal fulfilment. At no point does Dr LeShan violate his own scientific discipline or sensibilities. Yet at no point does he bind himself to scientific irrelevancies. Rather, he makes it clear that if the rich rewards of a meditative approach to life are to be discovered, the disciplined approach of the scientific mind must be employed even though the explorations move beyond familiar fields and clearly marked pathways.

Fortunately this is not a book merely to be read. It is an invitation to test the assumptions you have about life. It asks you to ask yourself how you use your mind and how you conceive your spirit. Then it asks that you test the premise of the book and do the hard work that is essential to discover the dormant or unused dimension of your own being to move toward the self-actualized, self-fulfilled person you might become. In that way you might well enjoy not only an important mental and spiritual experience, but also you might find that powerful therapeutic forces have been set at work in your life to change your view of yourself and your concept of the universe of which you are a part. Then the book will have fulfilled its purpose of making you a richer and more significant person. Then Dr LeShan will be able to do for you what he has done for many in his training programmes, discover the self you never knew existed.

EDGAR N. JACKSON
CORINTH, VERMONT

NOTES

Chapter 1

1. See, for example, W. R. Inge, *Christian Mysticism* (New York: Meridian Books, 1956), p. xvii.
2. C. D. Broad, *Religion, Philosophy and Psychical Research* (London: Routledge & Kegan Paul, 1953), p. 3.
3. Evelyn Underhill, *Mysticism*, 4th ed. (London: Methuen and Co., 1912), p. 254.
4. Alan W. Watts, *Psychotherapy East and West* (New York: Ballantine Books, 1968).

Chapter 2

1. Thomas Merton, *The Ascent to Truth* (New York: Viking, 1959), p. 185.

Chapter 3

1. The term 'understanding' has two meanings. In the usual, modern sense of the word it means to analyse the components of a situation or entity and to be able to describe the formal aspects of their interrelationships. This is an intellectual process. In the other, older sense of the word it means to 'stand under', to be a part of and – through this participation – to comprehend the entity or situation. It is a more complete, organismal process. The first definition is the one applying to physics' understanding of the problem. The second, as I shall describe, is more related to the mystic's understanding of his paradox. I am indebted to the philosopher Jacob Needleman for this clarification.
2. Lawrence LeShan, *Clairvoyant Reality* (Turnstone Press, 1980).
3. Josiah Royce, *The Conception of Immortality* (Boston: Houghton Mifflin & Co., 1900).
4. If anyone wishes to test this statement, I refer to a paper entitled 'Physicists and Mystics: Similarities in World View' in my book cited

above. In this, sixty-two statements of how the world works are printed. Half of them are from mystics, half from physicists. The game is to determine which persuasion the author of each followed. So similar are their viewpoints that so far no one has beaten the game.

5. Arthur Deikman, 'Experimental Meditation', in C. Tart, ed., *Altered States of Consciousness* (New York: Doubleday Anchor, 1972), pp. 204, 222.

Chapter 4

1. See, for example, F. N. Pitts, 'The Biochemistry of Anxiety', *Scientific American*, February 1969.
2. For those interested in a more detailed account, I suggest R. Keith Wallace and H. Benson, 'The Physiology of Meditation', *Scientific American*, February 1972; and C. Tart, ed., *Altered States of Consciousness* (New York: Doubleday Anchor, 1972).

Chapter 5

1. Werner Heisenberg, *Philosophic Problems of Nuclear Science* (Greenwich, Con.: Fawcett Premier, 1966), p. 82.
2. There are several books on this method that are well worth reading: E. Herregel, *Zen and the Art of Archery* and *Zen and the Art of Flower Arrangement*; and C. Humphreys, *The Way of Action* (Baltimore: Penguin, 1960). The first two are excellent autobiographical accounts of individuals who worked on the path of action through the skills of archery and of flower arranging. The third is a serious analysis of this method by the leading Buddhist of the Western world.

Chapter 6

1. I am following here the excellent analysis given by Claudio Naranjo in Claudio Naranjo and Robert Ornstein, *The Psychology of Meditation* (New York: Viking Press, 1971). This is one of the most useful and readable books in the field and I much recommend it.

Chapter 7

1. Humphrey Osmond, a psychiatrist who knows a great deal about the paranormal, once said that science is not made up of common sense, but uncommon sense.
2. There are a large number of books giving this data in overview and in detail. A few of the best include R. Heywood, *The Sixth Sense* (London: Pan Books, 1959); C. D. Broad, *Lectures in Psychical Research* (New York: Humanities Press, 1962); G. Murphy, *The Challenge of Psychical Research* (New York: Harper & Row, 1963).

In addition, anyone who wishes to read the hard-core experimental work as it is going on today can find it in *The Journal of the American Society for Psychical Research*.

3. For an intensive analysis of this state of consciousness, see Lawrence LeShan, *Toward a General Theory of the Paranormal* (New York: Parapsychology Foundation, 1969) or *Clairvoyant Reality* (Turnstone Press, 1980).

Chapter 8

1. Not only are there the objections to the path of the middle way discussed in Chapter 6, but I do not believe that exercises of this type should be done without a good teacher. There are too many possibilities for them to lead to negative results and bad feelings unless you have a good deal of experience in meditation or have an experienced guide.

2. The two kinds of benefit are not separate, as this discussion would seem to imply. It is a matter of emphasis on one aspect or the other, that is all. Meditation is one road, not two. The first part of meditation, which stresses the disciplining of the mind, is part of the path to deeper insights into reality and cannot be separated from it. This understanding is of gradual acquisition in spite of all the talk about sudden transformations. The second part of the meditation path, although it emphasizes the acquiring of this new viewpoint, also continues the disciplining and strengthening of the personality structure.

3. Philip Kapleau, *Three Pillars of Zen* (Boston: Beacon Press, 1968), pp. 113 ff.

4. E. Kadloubousky and G. E. H. Palmer, trans., *Writings from the Philokalia or Prayer of the Heart* (London: Faber and Faber, 1951), p. 90.

Chapter 9

1. Evelyn Underhill, *The Mystics of the Church* (New York: Schocken Books, 1964), p. 16.

2. See, for example, Nikos Kazantzakis, *Report to Greco* (New York: Simon and Schuster, 1965); Arthur Koestler, *The Lotus and the Robot* (New York: Macmillan, 1960); and Thomas Merton, *The Ascent to Truth* (New York: Viking Press, 1959).

3. George Santayana, *Reason in Science* (New York: Collier, 1962), p. 14.

4. Try reading this as a document of a mystical viewpoint some time. It is quite startling when you do. I am indebted to Dr Jacob Needleman for pointing this out to me. Plato's teacher, if not Plato himself, was trained in the Eleusinian mystical school.

5. Carl Jung said that this is so because the Indians never learned to really

think, to use scientific language. 'The Hindus', said Jung, 'are notoriously weak in rational exposition. They think for the most part in parables or images. They are not interested in reason. That, of course, is a basic condition of the Orient as a whole . . .

'So far as I can see, an Indian, so long as he remains an Indian, doesn't think – at least in the same way as we do. Rather he *perceives* a thought. In this way, the Indian approximates primitive ways of thinking. I don't say that the Indian is primitive, but merely that that the processes of his thought remind me of primitive methods of producing thoughts' (M. Serrano, *C. G. Jung and Hermann Hesse: A Record of Two Friendships*, New York: Schocken, 1966, pp. 50 ff.).

6. H. Margenau, 'Meaning and Scientific Status of Casuality', in S. Morgenbesser, *Philosophy of Science* (New York: Meridian, 1960), p. 436.
7. J. Krishnamurti, *The Brockwood Talks and Discussion* (Berkeley, Calif.: Shambala Publications, 1970).
8. Personal communication, 1970.
9. Jack Gariss, *A Beginner's Guide to Meditation* (Los Angeles: Mystic Circle, 1967).

Chapter 10

1. *The Autobiography of St Thérèse of Lisieux*, trans. J. Beevers (New York: Doubleday Image), p. 133.
2. *The Secret Oral Teachings in Tibetan Buddhist Sects*, trans. Alexandra David-Neel and Lama Yongdon (San Francisco: City Lights Book, 1967), pp. 7–8.
3. Columbia University, New York, April 16, 1973.
4. Thomas Merton, *Contemplative Prayer* (New York: Doubleday, 1969), p. 38.
5. Books that are particularly useful (and available today) for this part of the process include: Walter T. Stace, *Mysticism and Philosophy* (New York: Lippincott, 1960); Bertrand Russell, *Mysticism and Logic and Other Essays* (London: Longmans, Green; 1925); Evelyn Underhill, *Practical Mysticism* (London: J. M. Dent, 1914) and *Mysticism* (New York: Dutton, 1930); Lawrence LeShan, *Toward a General Theory of the Paranormal* (New York: Parapsychology Foundation, 1969) and *Clairvoyant Reality* (Turnstone Press, 1980); and Aldous Huxley, *The Perennial Philosophy* (New York: Meridian, 1970).
6. Carlos Castaneda, *The Teaching of Don Juan: A Yaqui Way of Knowledge* (New York: Ballantine, 1968), *A Separate Reality* (New York: Pocket Books, 1972), and *Journey to Ixtlan* (New York: Touchstone Books, 1972).

Chapter 11

1. Carl Rogers, 'Some Directions and End Points in Therapy', in O. H. Mowrer, ed., *Psychotherapy, Theory and Research* (New York: Ronald Press, 1953).
2. Thomas Merton, *The Wisdom of the Desert* (New York: New Directions, 1970), p. 26.
3. Pir Vilayat Khan, talk at Columbia University, New York, 1973.
4. Ibid.
5. Rogers, *On Becoming a Person* (Boston: Houghton Mifflin, 1961), p. 118.

Chapter 12

1. For a fuller description of this way of being in the world (and of the training seminars in psychic healing, mentioned above, which grew out of this research), see my *Clairvoyant Reality* (Turnstone Press, 1980).

Afterword

1. Jerome Frank, *Fate and Freedom* (Boston: Beacon Press, 1953), p. 164.
2. Harris Elliott Kirk, *Atoms, Men and God* (Chapel Hill: University of North Carolina Press, 1932), p. 37.
3. Edgar D. Adrian, *The Physical Basis of Mind* (London: Blackwell, 1957), pp. 7–10.
4. Ibid, p. 10.
5. John Calvin, *Institutes*, ed. John T. McNeill (Philadelphia: Westminster Press, 1960), Vol. 1, Chaps. 2, 6.
6. John Caird, in John Baille, *The Idea of Revelation in Recent Thought* (New York: Columbia University Press, 1956).
7. Baille, *Idea of Revelation*, p. 17.
8. Charles S. Sherrington, *Man on His Nature* (New York: Columbia University Press, 1951).
9. Fritz L. Kunz, *The Decline of Materialism* (Rye, N. Y.: Wainwright House, 1957), pp. 21–28.
10. Wayne E. Oates, *Religious Dimensions of Personality* (New York: Association Press, 1957), p. 177.
11. Ibid.
12. Nelson N. Foote and Leonard S. Cottrell, Jr., *Identity and Interpersonal Competence* (Chicago: University of Chicago Press, 1955), p. 57.
13. David Riesman, *Individualism Reconsidered* (Glencoe, Ill.: Free Press, 1954), p. 403.
14. Pitirim A. Sorokin, in Alson J. Smith, *Psychic Source Book* (New York: Creative Age Press, 1951), pp. v–viii.
15. Ibid.

16. Werner Heisenberg, *The Philosophical Problems of Nuclear Science* (New York: Pantheon, 1952), p. 158.
17. Edmund W. Sinnott. *The Biology of the Spirit* (New Haven: Yale University Press, 1955).
18. Bertrand Russell, *Mysticism and Logic* (New York: Anchor Books, 1957), p. 1.
19. Ibid.
20. Albert Einstein, *Out of My Later Years* (New York: Philosophical LIbrary, 1950), p. 26.
21. Paul Tillich, *Systematic Theology* (Chicago: University of Chicago Press, 1951–63), p. 110.

INDEX